T0068815

Slang: A Very Short Introduction

Very Short Introductions available now:

ACCOUNTING Christopher Nobes
ADVERTISING Winston Fletcher
AFRICAN AMERICAN RELIGION
    Eddie S. Glaude Jr.
AFRICAN HISTORY John Parker and
    Richard Rathbone
AFRICAN RELIGIONS Jacob K. Olupona
AGNOSTICISM Robin Le Poidevin
ALEXANDER THE GREAT
    Hugh Bowden
ALGEBRA Peter M. Higgins
AMERICAN HISTORY Paul S. Boyer
AMERICAN IMMIGRATION
    David A. Gerber
AMERICAN LEGAL HISTORY
    G. Edward White
AMERICAN POLITICAL HISTORY
    Donald Critchlow
AMERICAN POLITICAL PARTIES
    AND ELECTIONS L. Sandy Maisel
AMERICAN POLITICS
    Richard M. Valelly
THE AMERICAN PRESIDENCY
    Charles O. Jones
THE AMERICAN REVOLUTION
    Robert J. Allison
AMERICAN SLAVERY
    Heather Andrea Williams
THE AMERICAN WEST Stephen Aron
AMERICAN WOMEN'S HISTORY
    Susan Ware
ANAESTHESIA Aidan O'Donnell
ANARCHISM Colin Ward
ANCIENT ASSYRIA Karen Radner
ANCIENT EGYPT Ian Shaw

ANCIENT EGYPTIAN ART AND
    ARCHITECTURE Christina Riggs
ANCIENT GREECE Paul Cartledge
THE ANCIENT NEAR EAST
    Amanda H. Podany
ANCIENT PHILOSOPHY Julia Annas
ANCIENT WARFARE Harry Sidebottom
ANGELS David Albert Jones
ANGLICANISM Mark Chapman
THE ANGLO-SAXON AGE John Blair
THE ANIMAL KINGDOM
    Peter Holland
ANIMAL RIGHTS David DeGrazia
THE ANTARCTIC Klaus Dodds
ANTISEMITISM Steven Beller
ANXIETY Daniel Freeman and
    Jason Freeman
THE APOCRYPHAL GOSPELS
    Paul Foster
ARCHAEOLOGY Paul Bahn
ARCHITECTURE Andrew Ballantyne
ARISTOCRACY William Doyle
ARISTOTLE Jonathan Barnes
ART HISTORY Dana Arnold
ART THEORY Cynthia Freeland
ASTROBIOLOGY David C. Catling
ATHEISM Julian Baggini
AUGUSTINE Henry Chadwick
AUSTRALIA Kenneth Morgan
AUTISM Uta Frith
THE AVANT GARDE David Cottington
THE AZTECS David Carrasco
BACTERIA Sebastian G. B. Amyes
BARTHES Jonathan Culler
THE BEATS David Sterritt

Available soon:

For more information visit our website

www.oup.com/vsi/

Jonathon Green

SLANG

A Very Short Introduction

OXFORD
UNIVERSITY PRESS

OXFORD
UNIVERSITY PRESS

Great Clarendon Street, Oxford, OX2 6DP,
United Kingdom

Oxford University Press is a department of the University of Oxford.
It furthers the University's objective of excellence in research, scholarship,
and education by publishing worldwide. Oxford is a registered trade mark of
Oxford University Press in the UK and in certain other countries

Published in the United States of America by Oxford University Press
198 Madison Avenue, New York, NY 10016, United States of America

British Library Cataloguing in Publication Data

Data available

Library of Congress Control Number: 2015950354

ISBN 978-0-19-872953-2

Printed and bound by
CPI Group (UK) Ltd, Croydon, CR0 4YY

Contents

List of illustrations

The publisher and author apologize for any errors or omissions in the
above list. If contacted they will be pleased to rectify these at the earliest
opportunity.

Chapter 1
'Slang': the word

It is perhaps apt that the etymology of the word slang, like that of its French coeval *argot* (properly the jargon of the criminal milieu, but accepted as an effective equivalent of the English term) remains a problem.

It has its creation myths. Like all such confabulations they are undoubtedly unsound. That they come from the beliefs of what were once termed 'the dangerous classes' should be of no surprise. These purported origins involve a great leader and his community of criminal beggars and the establishment of codes both social and linguistic. In France it was *le Grand Coesre*, a word surely linked to Caesar, who gathers his followers and lays down the laws, including those of secret communication. In England it was one *Cock Lorel*, King of the Beggars, who performed the same office, bringing his people together at the pleasingly named Devil's Arse Peak in Derbyshire. However *cock lorel* means no more than what modernity would term a 'top villain', and we must accept that the myth, however appealing, is but a myth.

The slang lexicographer Eric Partridge termed it a 'prize problem word' and prizes or otherwise, the challenge persists. We are not helped by the delay in the printed appearance of the word itself. If we accept, with John Simpson, its present-day editor, that *The New Dictionary of the Canting Crew* of c.1698, known to users as 'B.E.' from the sole identification we have of its anonymous author, is 'the first slang dictionary', then the language it contains would still not be properly labelled for another sixty years. What remains the earliest recorded use of the word in the context of non-standard language is dated to a play of 1756.

There is, however, evidence through the 1740s of alternative senses, of which all are underpinned by some idea of duplicity: a line of work (first found in 1741), nonsense (1747), and, as a verb, to cheat, to swindle, to defraud (1741) and, the first suggestion of speech, to abuse or banter with (1749). There is also 'A Plan for a Hospital for Decayed Thief-Takers', a document attributed to the thief-taker and receiver Jonathan Wild, which contains the line: 'The master who teaches them should be a man well versed in the cant language, commonly called the Slang Patter, in which they should by all means excel.' Wild was hanged in 1725; the pamphlet is dated 1758. And while it was allegedly 'printed from a manuscript, said to be written by Jonathan Wild while under condemnation in Newgate,' its signature 'Henry Humbug' almost certainly suggests a later, satirical author. (Though to what extent, given the paucity of cites, cant was 'commonly called the Slang Patter' even in 1758 remains debatable. The next such use is not found until a ballad of the 1780s and as a verb to *patter slang* is unrecorded until 1827, and that in Australia among the transportees.)

Citations for *slang* remain limited in the 18th century, and the word remained ignored by lexicography. The British publisher, pornographer, and slang collector John Camden Hotten, who was the first to look hard at the question, offered this round-up in his *Slang Dictionary* (1859):

> The word Slang is only mentioned by two lexicographers
> Webster and Ogilvie. Johnson, Walker, and the older compilers of
> dictionaries give 'slang' as the preterite [i.e. a past tense] of 'sling,'
> but not a word about Slang in the sense of low, vulgar, or

unrecognised language. The origin of the word has often been asked for in literary journals and books, but only one man, until recently, ever hazarded an etymology Jonathan Bee. With a recklessness peculiar to ignorance, Bee stated that Slang was derived from 'the slangs or fetters worn by prisoners, having acquired that name from the manner in which they were worn, as they required a sling of string to keep them off the ground'.

Hotten's own belief was that,

> Slang is not an English word; it is the Gipsy term for their secret language, and its synonym is Gibberish another word which was believed to have had no distinct origin.

Since then the term has been subjected to continued analysis, either by professional or independent scholars, and one can discern three groups of theories: (1) Romani; (2) Scandinavian; (3) variations on SE (Standard English) *language* or *lingo* or French *langue*. A fourth group, least likely, contains those most kindly labelled 'optimistic'.

Romani

The basis for this attribution lies in Isaac Taylor's assertion of 'a village called Flash' found 'in a wild district of Derbyshire'. Here were gypsy squatters, who took the name 'Flash men' and called their jargon 'Flash talk' (Figure 1). He noted that a *slang* was a narrow strip of land, such as used for gypsy encampments. To be 'out on the slang' was to travel the country as a hawker whose temporary camp would be on a slang. A travelling show, run and frequented by gypsies, was also a *slang*. The move to slang meaning language seemed logical. The phrase *slang patter* (i.e. 'camp language') was seen as underpinning the belief. Setting aside the fanciful village (Taylor appears to been confused by *flash*, the variety of slang coined and popularized by 18th-century rakes and other 'sportsmen', itself based on the standard English

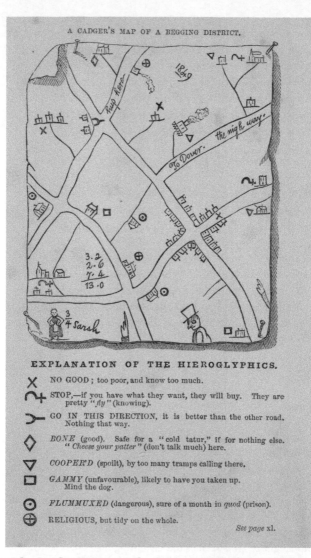

A CADGER'S MAP OF A BEGGING DISTRICT.

EXPLANATION OF THE HIEROGLYPHICS.

✗   NO GOOD ; too poor, and know too much.

⚻   STOP,—if you have what they want, they will buy. They are pretty "*fly*" (knowing).

⅄   GO IN THIS DIRECTION, it is better than the other road. Nothing that way.

◇   *BONE* (good). Safe for a "cold tatur," if for nothing else. "*Cheese your patter*" (don't talk much) here.

▽   *COOPER'D* (spoilt), by too many tramps calling there.

▢   *GAMMY* (unfavourable), likely to have you taken up. Mind the dog.

⊙   *FLUMMUXED* (dangerous), sure of a month in *quod* (prison).

⊕   RELIGIOUS, but tidy on the whole.

See page xl.

1. John Camden Hotten: a Cadger's (i.e. wandering beggar's) Map (1859). These covered local areas and used commonly understood signs to indicate their characteristics as regarded the possibilities, or otherwise, of successful begging.

4

meaning of ostentation; there may also be links to the
16th-century meeting of England's criminal vagrants noted
above). Meanwhile, it has proved impossible to find a Romani
origin for *slang*.

Scandinavian

The Oxford philologist Walter Skeat, whose *Etymological
Dictionary of the English Language* had appeared between 1879
and 1882, and who in turn took his examples from his predecessor
Hensleigh Wedgwood, one of the pioneers of the *New* and
subsequently *Oxford English Dictionary* (*OED*), attributed *slang*
unequivocally to the Scandinavian languages. Listing such
terms as the Norwegian *sleng*, 'a slinging, an invention, device,
strategem... a little addition or burthen of a song, in verse and
melody'; *ettersleng* (lit. 'afterslang'), 'a burthen at the end of
a verse or ballad'; *slengjenamn*, a nickname; *slengjeord*, an
insulting word or allusion; the Icelandic *slyngr* and *slunginn*, well
versed in, cunning; and the Swedish *slanger*, to gossip, Skeat was
certain 'that all the above Norwegian and Icelandic words are
derivatives from "sling" is quite clear... I see no objection to this
explanation.' Other etymologists tended to follow Skeat. Henry
Bradley who succeeded Sir James Murray as editor of the *OED* in
1915, accepted the Norwegian connection. So too did Professors
Ernest Weekley and H. C. Wyld in subsequent studies. More
recently Eric Partridge modified the Norwegian thesis in his own
etymological dictionary. For him *slang* is a dialect past participle
of the verb *sling*, which has its roots in Old and Middle English
and links to Old Norse, thus giving the concept of 'slung' or
'thrown' language. This conveniently encompasses the abusive
side of slang, e.g. 'sling off at' and is duly bolstered by the
Norwegian *slenga keften* (also cited by Skeat) lit. to 'sling the jaw',
and thus, literally, to use slang, as well as Skeat's *slengjeord*.

Sir William Craigie, dealing with *slang* for the *OED* took that
Dictionary's usual cautious view on such matters: it was 'a word of

cant origin, the ultimate source of which is not apparent'; Craigie compounded his rejection of possible origins with a further note: 'the date and early associations of the word make it unlikely that there is any connection with certain Norwegian forms in *sleng-* which exhibit some approximation in sense'. This (in spring 2015) remains the *OED*'s position: 'etymology unknown'.

Language, lingo, and *langue*

Given that slang, whether as criminal jargon or general vulgarity, is incontrovertibly a language, a link to SE *language* or *lingo*, usually seen as slightly negative, or French *langue* is hard to resist. One inescapable question remained: why the 's'? This was justified in some theories by the linguistic theory of 'attraction', whereby a compound term is incorrectly divided and one half creates a new word. In this case supposed compounds such as 'beggars' lang' or 'thieves' lang' had moved the 's' and created slang. The absence of any such compounds has been considered sufficient to explode the theory, although one might suggest a faint link in the modern assertion, however much rejected, of an origin in *secret lang*uage.

Other theories

The elision of *secret lang*uage aside, there have been many more or less ingenious suggestions. As noted by Hotten his predecessor Jon Bee linked the use of *slangs* = fetters (taken in turn from Dutch *slang* = a snake) to the speech of those who endured them; there is the Dutch General *Slangenburg, fl.* 1700, known for his abuse of his rival the Duke of Marlborough. Another elaborate theory devolves upon the reordering of the Hebrew לשן (*LSN*), meaning language. None work.

A solution?

Although at time of writing the unrevised *OED* remains unconvinced, the nearest possibility to a solution has been suggested by Prof. Anatoly Liberman. Noting clues in Taylor, in Barrère and Leland's *Slang, Jargon and Cant* (1889–90), and in a little-noticed article by John Sampson in the *Chester Courant* (1898) which stresses the absence of any links to Romani, while noting the importance of a *slang* or strip of land, he sees it thus.

The roots do indeed lie in Scandinavian words, but while such terms may also mean throw or fling, the focus should be on their parallel definitions: to wander, walk aimlessly, or stroll. These include Norwegian *slenge*, 'hang loose, dangle, wobble...blurt out words' and Danish *slaenge* 'wave arms; swing, hang loose'. 'Their common denominator seems to be "move freely in any direction".' He then posits a 'prepositional phrase **pa slaenget*...''(out) on the slang''. **Slaenget* [an asterisk * indicates a supposed, but unproven root word] must have meant the gang's turf' (from Danish *slaeng*/ Norwegian *sleng*, a gang or band). 'Those who travelled about the country or a certain area were thus "on the slang".' (This parallels *argot*, which meant 'wandering hawkers' before it meant their language.) He notes that 'verbs of movement designating wandering have the tendency to associate themselves with the name of the territory in which the movement occurs'. So 'we have *slang* "long narrow piece of land" and Scots *slanger* "linger, go slowly" presumably from **slenge*, wander, loaf. The slang must have been the land over which one wandered.'

Such terms may have been known in the North of England and may never have entered standard English, but were adopted by hawkers, and then popularized within the London underworld. A hawkers' licence is found as 'a slang' and to travel as a hawker was to 'go out on the slang'. The linguistic development is thus: a piece of land (strip of field/wayside gypsy encampment) → those who travel along regular routes (hawkers) → the speech they use → the speech used by those 'outside the law'. The shift in slang's primary meaning of 'vagrant jargon' to 'vulgar speech' may be attributed to the long-established assumption that if slang is used by those outside social respectability it must be categorized as being outside the linguistic equivalent.

All this seems to stand up linguistically. The problem, if it exists, is evidentiary. There is no recorded example prior to the 19th century of *slang* meaning a licence. This is found in 1812, meaning a licence to travel or a legal warrant, and only in the 1864 edition of Hotten is it specifically defined as a hawker's licence. Yet there were records of licences in earlier texts. Harman's 'beggar book' the *Caveat for Common Cursetours* (1566) lists a *gybe*, often counterfeited, which was embellished by a *jark* or seal. Both terms occur regularly. The early 17th century gives *tickrum* or *tick-Rome*, which seems to mean a 'ticket' provided by 'Rome', i.e. London as being the seat of authority. We can accept that far from every hawkers' term was collected, but if 16th-century hawkers used *slang* as a licence, it seems to have lain very low. Hotten also lists 'on the slang'. Prior to that the phrase is very rare and yields two citations, one of 1741 where it occurs as 'on the slango' and the other, of 1789, in a confected conversation between two fictional villains, in which it suggests criminality in general, rather than begging.

The nature of slang—the marginal speech of marginal individuals—naturally makes its recording problematic. Especially in its earliest period. Nonetheless, hard evidence is important, and the establishment of a concrete etymology remains frustrated by its absence.

Chapter 2
'Slang' as a linguistic register

If the etymology of slang remains debatable, its definitions, while wide-ranging and continually upgraded by amateurs and professionals alike, follow a reasonably well-trodden path. It indicates a marginal, contrarian lexis, created and largely used by those beyond the social, and by extension linguistic, pale. Its use may have become more extensive alongside the more relaxed social mores of contemporary speech, but it continues to offend language purists and while their condemnations are no longer quite so unyielding as was once the case, it remains tainted by its criminal and underclass associations.

First used in fiction, a play, in 1756, entered into a dictionary (Webster's *American*) in 1828, and noted thereafter by the lexicographers, 'slang' as a word within the English language, serving to specify a particular linguistic register, was set firmly amid respectable speech by the *OED* in a section published in September 1911. Since then it remains essentially unchanged as to its definitions and in its use, even if it continues to develop as a vocabulary. The philologists and lexicographers remain generally consistent in their opinions. Since the *OED* laid down lexicographical law they may have replaced simple definition by more complex explanations, but ultimately they differ only in the nuances.

The definitions of slang

If there exists a standard, of whatever sort, there seems to be an innate human desire to create an alternative and language is surely no exception. Hotten, as keen as any other Victorian scholar to find antecedents in the classical and pre-classical worlds, offers the readers of his *Slang Dictionary* (1859) an alluring, if somewhat fantastical picture of this 'universal and ancient' species of language:

> If we are to believe implicitly the saying of the wise man, that 'there is nothing new under the sun' the 'fast' men of buried Nineveh, with their knotty and door-matty looking beards, may have cracked Slang jokes on the steps of Sennacherib's palace; and the stones of Ancient Egypt, and the bricks of venerable and used up Babylon, may, for aught we know, be covered with slang hieroglyphics unknown to modern antiquarians...

Perhaps. We might well wish it so but we shall never know. That the Greeks and Romans had slang we can be sure. Latin literature, for instance, offers images for sexual intercourse, the vagina, and the penis, which foreshadow those of modern slang. Just as we find today, the penis is characterized as a sharp or pointed instrument, a weapon, a household object, one of a variety of agricultural implements, or a tool; it can be a pole or stake; it uses personification and animal and anatomical metaphors and is represented as a man's 'private' property. This, undoubtedly, is something we can recognize.

But we must be careful: all this is literary, and of spoken Latin, street Latin, we know nothing. We must accept that for all the parallel imagery this is not slang, any more than certain terms to be found in Chaucer or *Piers Plowman* qualify as terms from a register that would not be acknowledged for four more centuries.

As a word that describes a form of speech *slang* only emerges into the (printed) language in the mid-18th century. The *OED* (1933 and unrevised at the time of writing), which included mainly that slang terminology which occurred in literature, in the 16th and 17th century glossarists and in certain slang dictionaries, defined the term as 'The special vocabulary used by any set of persons of a low or disreputable character; language of a low a vulgar type,' and adds somewhat circuitously, 'Language of a highly colloquial type, considered as below the level of standard educated speech, and consisting either of new words or of current words employed in some special sense' (*colloquial* being defined as 'Belonging to common speech; characteristic of or proper to ordinary conversation, as distinguished from formal or elevated language'). The word is so far first recorded in 1756, when in Act I of William Toldervy's play *The History of the Two Orphans* one finds, 'Thomas Throw had been upon the town, knew the slang well...and understood every word in the scoundrel's dictionary.' But this slang is not defined. Was Throw's 'slang' a reference to his speech, or to a duplicitous and probably criminal way of conducting himself? That he knew 'the slang' and 'the scoundrel's dictionary' may or may not have also confirmed that he used it. And if we assume that 'the slang' is that lexis recorded in 'the scoundrel's dictionary' does this not suggest that it is no more than a synonym for *cant*, or criminal jargon, and does not involve the more general sense of today? As ever, slang challenges those who seek to pin it down.

As time passes and definitions pile up the mood is one of gradual softening. There is a movement from absolute dismissal, on the basis of slang's criminal users, towards a wider acknowledgement of slang as simply 'vulgar', that is as used by the common speaker, and thence as no more than a non-standard subset of English as a whole. By the time we reach the 21st century slang is seen as much as flippant, colourful, or irreverent as anything else. Criminality is no longer a given, nor, at least as spelled out, is an automatic association with the working class. The key term 'low', whether applied to the language or its speakers, has been abandoned.

In the end the best assessment may be that posited by Bethany K. Dumas and Jonathan Lighter in their 1978 essay 'Is Slang a Word for Linguists?': 'Annoyance and frustration await anyone who searches the professional literature for a definition or even a conception of slang that can stand up to scrutiny. Instead one finds impressionism, much of it of a dismaying kind.' And of all the definitions on offer there is much to be said for Lighter's own synthesis, in the *Cambridge History of the English Language* (2001, vol. vi: N. America):

> So taking into account the various definitions in dictionaries as well as the more detailed treatments of such authors as Henry Bradley, Stuart Flexner ... H. L. Mencken, and Eric Partridge, the following definition will be stipulated ... : Slang denotes an informal, nonstandard, nontechnical vocabulary composed chiefly of novel-sounding synonyms (and near synonyms) for standard words and phrases; it is often associated with youthful, raffish, or undignified persons and groups; and it conveys often striking connotations of impertinence or irreverence, especially for established attitudes and values within the prevailing culture.

What is 'slang'?

Yet if we know, thanks to so many scholars, what *slang* is as a register, slang's innate slipperiness, its multi-faceted tricksiness, means that faced with a given term it is far from simple for the lexicographer to assign it as 'slang'. That the *OED* was forced to define one register, *slang*, in terms of another, *colloquial*, points up the problem. Etymology and definition aside, we must still ask: what qualifies as slang. And what does not. Neither linguists nor lexicographers made a serious attempt to deal with this, until in

1933, Eric Partridge, writing in his pioneering overview *Slang To-day and Yesterday*, offered some seventeen criteria which might make a word slang. Julie Coleman, in her history *The Story of Slang* (2012), has reduced the qualifications to eleven. Jonathan Lighter and Bethany Dumas cut them down to four. Yet in answering their own question, Lighter and Dumas have made it clear that slang cannot be shoehorned into seventeen, let alone four sizes fit all.

In 1933 some of Partridge's suggestions claimed that 'slang is employed':

(1) In sheer high spirits, by the young in heart as well as by the young in years; 'just for the fun of the thing'; in playfulness or waggishness.

(2) As an exercise either in wit and ingenuity or in humour. (The motive behind this is usually self-display or snobbishness, emulation or responsiveness, delight in virtuosity.)

(3) To be 'different', to be novel.

(4) To be picturesque (either positively or—as in the wish to avoid insipidity—negatively).

...

(6) To escape from clichés, or to be brief and concise. (Actuated by impatience with existing terms.)

...

(8) To lend an air of solidity, concreteness, to the abstract; of earthiness to the idealistic; of immediacy and appositeness to the remote. (In the cultured the effort is usually premeditated, while in the uncultured it is almost always unconscious when it is not rather subconscious.)

...

(10) To speak or write down to an inferior, or to amuse a superior public; or merely to be on a colloquial level with either one's audience or one's subject matter.

(11) For ease of social intercourse. (Not to be confused or merged with the preceding.)

Four decades after Partridge Jonathan Lighter and Bethany Dumas suggested that 'an expression should be regarded as true slang if it meets at least two of the following criteria':

1. Its presence will markedly lower, at least for the moment, the dignity of formal or serious speech or writing...
2. Its use implies the user's special familiarity either with the referent or with that less statusful or less responsible class of people who have such special familiarity and use the term....
3. It is a tabooed term in ordinary discourse with persons of higher social status or greater responsibility....
4. It is used in place of the well-known conventional synonym, especially in order (a) to protect the user from the discomfort caused by the conventional item or (b) to protect the user from the discomfort or annoyance of further elaboration.

Such 'rules', reverse engineered from recorded slang use, are valid, but few slang users would pause to analyse their speech in this way. Academic theory suggests that users choose their slang but they do not. Criminal coinages, and such artificial creations as rhyming or back slang, may represent conscious coinages, but for most slang users, this is to assume a decision that is not there.

Some users, those for whom slang is simply one more fashionable accessory, may use it consciously, but most do not. Their slang use is transparent. It is there, it is the way they talk. One may interrogate, say, an engineer and uncover the jargon that they use for professional communications; fieldwork on the street is more difficult. 'What slang?' says the user. They may never use a standard word or phrase, but for them slang *is* the standard. This is not to deny a learning curve, as in any form of communication, and that may be dictated by the norms of the group with whom one wishes to be associated, but no one is thinking 'slang', simply 'that is what I/we call...' It is rather, as Mads Holmsgaard Eriksen, in a study on 'Translating the use of slang' prepared as a thesis for Aarhus University in 2010 and paraphrasing the American slang lexicologist Michael Adams, puts it, 'a set of words and expressions in a given language used to create group dynamics'. The problem for members of such groups begins when they move beyond their 'normal' environment and into the wider world. Slang fluency becomes standard inarticulacy and it is that perception that stands behind regular criticisms of the lexis, especially as tied into the currently dominant form of slang—that found in rap music—as underpinning illiteracy, joblessness, street crime, and even riots.

With rap in mind it is necessary to address an aspect of criticism that hitherto has been spared slang: its cheerful, flaunted denial of any vestige of that form of contemporary socio linguistic politeness known, whether advocated or demonized, as 'political correctness'. In an era of identity politics slang makes no attempt to vote. It remains racist, homophobic, and, of course, both sexist and misogynistic. It despises the tortured contrivances of gender identity. The briefest glance at the lexis will make it clear that such has been slang's policy throughout its recorded existence, but it is only relatively recently that such terminology has been seen as unacceptable by those who might otherwise be unfazed by a parallel part of the lexis: what others might condemn as 'dirty' words. Rap, and its West Indian peer dancehall, are particularly susceptible to such attacks, with the former seen as especially contemptuous of women and the latter focused on decrying homosexuals. Neither can be condemned as racist, although the unrestrained use of the word *nigger* offends all parties. That a number of artists are women does not seem to change the status quo: slang's male, heterosexual gaze is unflinching. If this is not compounded by 'white' that exclusion is mitigated by the predominant role of black performers, but for all the ostensible 'revolution' proclaimed in many lyrics, the language is, if such a concept is feasible, very much that of 'establishment' slang. Whether on *bee-atch* or *batty-boy*, slang long since declared open season.

What you hear is what you get

'Slang is a poor man's poetry,' suggested John Moore in *You English Words* (1962). The same sentiment underpins the title of Michael Adams's study *Slang: The People's Poetry* (2009). And like the poor, to whom must be attributed credit for the coinage, or at least the popularization of a major portion of its vocabulary, slang is always with us. Whether, as one observer suggests, it is the working man of language, doing the lexicon's 'dirty work' or, as Moore and Adams imply, it represents the lyrical creativity of the disenfranchised or, as its many critics still proclaim, it has nothing but the most deleterious effects on 'proper speech', slang remains a law unto itself.

For all the criteria, for all the inconsistent yet ultimately similar definitions, one is left, like the judge who knows pornography but still cannot say exactly what it is, as knowing it when one meets it. Like that other imponderable, humour, which like sex plays so central a role in slang, it is an empty vessel into which any and everyone can pour the filling of choice. Michael Adams, whose own interest in slang began with his study of the language used in the TV show *Buffy the Vampire Slayer* (*Slayer Slang*, 2003) agrees: 'Slang is what it is. You'll know it when you hear it.' For him much is down to context and the need to create a social link to those with whom one is speaking. Simply checking a dictionary definition, let alone multiple definitions, offers no help. As fellow slang expert Connie Eble puts it: 'Slang cannot be defined independent of its functions and use.' And both cite James B. McMillan from 1978:

> The basic problem of slang lexicology—definition of the class—has not been solved… Until slang can be objectively identified and segregated (so that dictionaries will not vary in labeling particular lexemes and idioms) or until more precise subcategories replace the catchall label SLANG, little can be done to analyze linguistically this kind of lexis.

Cant

The first systematic collections of non-standard language deal
with the insider language, effectively a jargon, of criminals. This
was and properly remains known as cant. The term comes from
the Latin *cantare*, to sing, and referred initially to the tones of
those clergy who, seen as insufficiently pious, delivered the mass
in sing-song tones. The same tones were associated with the voices
of importuning vagabonds. The language of crime naturally
persists, albeit with its vocabulary much altered, but the term
itself is rarely found outside technical, language-related use.
'Criminal slang' is the general name.

Cant, as in empty if enthusiastic but hypocritical pietism, is linked
to a specific 18th-century preacher rather than to villains, but the
19th century saw a blending of both senses to underpin certain
dismissals of words that were not 'slang' but rather linguistic
posing. The attack on 'slang' in *Household Words* (see 'Occupational
slang: jargon' below) was very much of that nature. In 1913 the
New International Dictionary, presumably seeking to offer clarity
in its definition of 'slang', only confused the issue:

> Originally, cant of thieves, gypsies, beggars, etc.; now, language or
> words consisting either of new words or phrases, often of the
> vagrant or illiterate classes, or of ordinary words or phrases in
> arbitrary senses, and having a conventional but vulgar or inelegant
> use; also, the jargon of a particular calling or class of society;
> popular cant.

Rhyming slang

Aside from the arrival of the lexis of recreational drug use, and
the slang that evolved from the two world wars, rhyming slang is
the register's great 'modern' invention. Hotten suggests that the
language was deliberately covert and was created by street

patterers to confuse the police who had, by now, decoded the older slang of the 18th-century villain. Another theory ascribes the original rhyming slang to thieves, whose varieties of slang had by necessity always been at the cutting edge of 'counter-language' coinage. Peter Wright, in *Cockney Dialect and Slang* (1981) adds bricklayer's slang (quoting a source who notes it to have been 'the most picturesque, involved and unintelligible' of all rhyming slangs); in addition he suggests a large input from the Irish navvies, recently imported to England to build railways and canals. According to its main lexicographer Julian Franklyn it was the linguistic rivalry between these navvies and the Cockneys (Figure 2) who worked alongside them and like them revelled in language, that created rhyming slang. There is no hard-and-fast answer, but the style seems to have developed around 1820–30 and was sufficiently common to have been included in slang dictionaries from 1857 onwards.

There is nothing mysterious about rhyming slang. It can, of course, defeat the untutored listener—its seeming impenetrability residing in its generally 'clipped' form, i.e. 'Barnet' for hair (rather than the full-out 'Barnet Fair'), but the basic principle is an undaunting one. One takes a word one wishes to describe, and in its place provides a brief phrase, usually of two but often of three words, of which the last word rhymes with the word for which it is a synonym. However, given the usual clipping of all but the first element, the rhyme, it might be said, becomes a technicality. This clipping, it should be stressed, is not a product of familiarity, the full phrase has not, as it were, 'worn away': it has been intrinsic to rhyming slang since its creation.

It remains popular; some indeed equate it with 'slang' *tout court*. Its lexis has created around 3,000 terms in all. Initially these were based on standard words—*apples and pears*: stairs, *saucepan lids*: kids—but it gradually embraced well-known proper names, usually of popular entertainers and more recently sports stars.

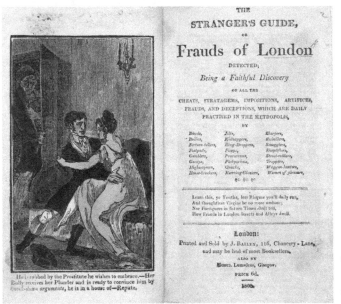

THE
STRANGER'S GUIDE,
OR
Frauds of London
DETECTED;

Being a Faithful Discovery

OF ALL THE

CHEATS, STRATAGEMS, IMPOSITIONS, ARTIFICES,
FRAUDS, AND DECEPTIONS, WHICH ARE DAILY
PRACTISED IN THE METROPOLIS,

BY

Bawds,	Jilts,	Sharpers,
Bullies,	Kidnappers,	Swindlers,
Fortune-tellers,	Ring-Droppers,	Smugglers,
Footpads,	Fops,	Shoplifters,
Gamblers,	Procuresses,	Street-robbers,
Gossips,	Pickpockets,	Trappers,
Highwaymen,	Quacks,	Waggon-hunters,
House-breakers,	Running-Glaziers,	Women of pleasure,

&c. &c. &c.

Learn this, ye Youths, less Risques you'll daily run,
And thoughtless Virgins be no more undone;
Nor Foreigners in future Times shall tell,
How Frauds in London Streets and Alleys dwell.

London:
Printed and Sold by J. BAILEY, 116, Chancery - Lane,
and may be had of most Booksellers,

ALSO BY

Messrs. Lumsden, Glasgow,

PRICE 6d.

1808.

He is robbed by the Prostitute he wishes to embrace.—Her
Bully receives her Plunder and is ready to convince him by
knock-down arguments, he is in a house of—Repute.

2. *The Strangers Guide or Frauds of London Detected* (1808). There were many such 'guides', but whether other tourists found them more useful than this unfortunate young man seems to have done is unknown.

This seems to have become the default for new coinages, and the use of one's name for such slang has become a rite of passage for footballers, TV and film stars, and similar celebrities.

Rhyming slang is seen as quintessentially British and even more so that of Cockney Londoners, but it has moved further afield. Setting aside its continuing popularity in Scotland, its first port of call would be Australia, where it took off around 1890. The vocabulary runs to around 650 terms and continues to add more. Rhyming slang's arrival in the USA came not too long after its appearance in the UK, and its first example was found in an issue of the *National Police Gazette* in 1859. In a move that seems bizarre in hindsight, rhyming slang was known then and for many decades as 'Australian slang'. The belief, however erroneous, seems to have originated in the arrival, especially on the West Coast, of a number of Australian criminals, keen to enjoy the rich pickings of the Gold Rush of 1849. At the same time or soon afterwards, rhyming slang began to be seen in Chicago and in New York. In these two cities it was more likely that the users were native American criminals (although some of the late 19th and early 20th century's most successful confidence tricksters, operating all over America, were Australians—not to mention the occasional Britisher), and the regular visits of British sailors to port cities must have left its linguistic legacy. The style was never very popular but America has yet to abandon rhyming slang. There are relatively few examples, perhaps half as many as there are Australian terms, but they exist, and readers of modern US crime novels will stumble upon them.

Backslang

Of the subsets of slang backslang is the shortest lived. Coined around the same time as was rhyming slang, and confined mainly to market-traders, it was created to be deliberately confusing. It must also have been hard to pronounce, as seen in the lists of backslanged coins and numbers in Hotten's dictionaries. Perhaps the only survivor is *yob*, i.e. boy. (Its demise, however, is restricted to the Anglophone world; *verlan*, from *l'invers*: reverse, remains a force within French *argot*, while *lunfardo*, the slang of Buenos Aires, also reverses syllables.) Its primary use seems to have been for counting: *yeneps* were pennies, *gens* were shillings and a run of numbers, also reversed, would be combined with them, e.g. *exis-evif gens*: six times five shillings or £1 10s. Backslang in turn spawned its own subset: butcher's backslang (again there is a French equivalent, *louchebem*, i.e. a back-slanged version of *boucher*). Like its creator it has virtually disappeared, though one very occasionally hears such terms as *feeb*, i.e. beef.

Occupational slang: jargon

Like cant, jargon, which originally referred to the twittering of birds, offers parallel meanings. On the one hand is the deliberately obfuscatory terminology of institutions, typically governments or major corporations. On the other is the specific slang, as opposed to the technical terms, of those involved in particular occupations. And like cant, jargon can be taken out of its proper context and used erroneously to describe slang in general.

In September 1856 Dickens's weekly *Household Words* attacked what was termed slang. It was everywhere and the journal offered lists to prove it. However aside from terms for 'drunk', 'money', and certain areas of criminality, the primary target is verbal affectation: in fashionable life, parliament, the law, and the stage. The words that have accrued to these and presumably other niche pursuits, whether seen as jobs or not. If this is slang it is occupational, and as such should better be categorized as jargon. This overlap was hardly new and it continues. The 'civilian' slang that is included in B.E.'s *New Dictionary of the Canting Crew* (*c.*1698) or Francis Grose's *Classical Dictionary of the Vulgar Tongue* (1785) is mainly that of specific professions; successive slang lexicographers have chosen to do the same, especially as regards the language of the forces. It is a hard call: is drug slang, which could be termed 'job-specific', jargon or, since so many people use drugs, just a part of the mainstream and as valid there as the language of drink? The choice seems to be down to the individual dictionary-maker.

Obscenities

As rhyming slang has come to be seen by many as the embodiment of slang, but in fact represents a very small proportion of its vocabulary, its twin, equally promoted as slang's primary ingredient, is the micro-lexis that contains the obscenities, the 'dirty words'. The reality is that such canonical terms as exist are very few in number—less than twenty—and while slang does indeed offer what some would see as a disproportionate focus on sex and defecation, and those parts of the body that are involved in both, its lengthy lists of synonyms for each are ultimately euphemistic. Nonetheless one finds these references from the earliest glossaries onwards. In the context of sex the terms draw on standard English, on puns, on euphemism, on nature and animals, and on foreign languages. In most cases the woman is passive, even invisible; the idea of physical domination by the male is a constant. In that of defecation, the process is somewhat slower: many of the basic terms were used for some time without comment. But the 'cleansing' of the English language during the 18th century drove them from the mainstream. Unsurprisingly, they found a way to the slang dictionaries. Modernity is less squeamish on either count and terms from both areas are far more common in speech, print, and other media. They remain, however, tainted by association with a less permissive past, and they are still firmly listed as slang.

Chapter 3
Is slang a language?

The general assumption is that slang is a language. More than one book has been titled 'slanguage' and the image is that of an established, if unconventional form of communication.

If a means of communication is a language then slang is surely such, and as much as any other lexical subset—jargon, technicalities, regionalisms—a part of the overarching English language. As such it may be considered as being on equal terms with standard English, the language, traditionally, of the broadsheet press, news broadcasters, and other top-down communicators. It is very likely not spoken in the cadences of what is locally seen as received pronunciation, but that does not disqualify it. Slang may be considered 'worse' than standard English and suffers such slipshod condemnations as 'bad' language or 'swear-words', but a more objective view would attribute such dismissals to prejudice rather than fact, still tarring the lexis with its origins in criminality. If the subsets of English represent a family, then slang might be seen as a cousin, a somewhat raffish and rackety one no doubt, but in no way a poor relation nor a black sheep.

But that does not answer the question in linguistic terms. Is it really a language? Or no more than an aggregation of words?

A lexis. A vocabulary. To couple its primary ingredient with the main arena in which it occurs, is it not just the words on (or in or of) the street?

If a language demands the fulfilment of certain rules—pronunciation, word order, grammar—then no, it is not. It is marginal, used by the marginal, expresses marginality. Those who use it may see it as a language, but on this basis they may equally well be wrong. That posited etymology, the *s* for 'secret' and *lang* for 'language', suggests that the belief is deep. But that suggested etymology is wrong too. It may be, or rather may have been, secret, but no matter; it still fails the tests that render it a fully fledged language. What it is, perhaps, is a lexis of synonymy. There are themes—topics it embraces, the philosophy of its use ('counter'/'subversive')—but even if it demands dictionaries, it is not a language as such.

Yet with all that said, the diagram with which Sir James Murray, its first editor, prefaced the *OED*, setting linguistic groupings around a central core, does equate slang with jargon/technical terms/dialect/etc. as equally valuable subsets of the overriding 'English language' (Figure 3).

The current *OED* (entry revised in 2008) offers this under language:

> Definition 1.a. The system of spoken or written communication used by a particular country, people, community, etc., typically consisting of words used within a regular grammatical and syntactic structure.

In that case, no. It is not a system. Nor, even if Victor Hugo wrote, in *The Hunchback of Notre Dame*, of 'the kingdom of argot' and even imagined a lengthy, vivid description of its 'citizens' parading through 15th-century Paris, and playwrights such as Thomas

3. An infographic provided by James Murray for the introduction of the *OED*'s first edition (1928). All varieties of English radiate from a common centre, slang is no less eligible than the rest.

Dekker and Ben Jonson rendered visible a 'beggar's brotherhood', is it a community. But let us look further:

> Definition 2. a. The form of words in which something is communicated; manner or style of expression.

Slang surely qualifies. And here the *OED* even cross-references to 'slangism' and 'slanguage' and notes 'freq. in bad language: coarse or offensive expressions'.

I write from a lexicographer's point of view, and am loathe to enter the complex world of linguistics. However, these two opposed but complementary definitions seem to echo the difference between what Ferdinand de Saussure labelled *langue* and *parole*: literally *language* and *speaking*. The former demands abstract concepts, systematic rules and conventions, and exists independently of the independent speaker. The latter is, in the simplest form, the way individuals speak, the way they use that language. Where *langue* is abstract and general, *parole* is concrete and specific. Slang, in the wider context of English, Murray's 'Common', seems to represent parole. It is very much tied, if not to individuals, then to relatively limited groups, it works against the background of the greater *langue*—the bulk of slang being examples of the way in which one may play with the standard lexis—but its vocabulary, as found in texts and collected in dictionaries, is pure *parole*. Those who collect the headwords of such dictionaries are invariably working backwards from what has been recorded, supposed representations of slang used 'live'. If there is a circularity here—the dictionary takes from the users, the users in turn may extract from the dictionary—it is inevitable and hardly restricted to slang. Despite some scholars' efforts to rein slang in, and they have been limited to attempting the creation of limits as to what 'is' and 'is not' slang, there is no slang grammar. Its ludic essence militates against such constraints. Frank Sechrist, writing of *The Psychology of Non-Standard Language* (1912), equated its inventiveness with 'the genius of language'. Genius or not, this linguistic playfulness does seem to be hard-wired. As Sechrist puts it:

The language which expresses the excitement of the market, the games of chance, the pursuit of wealth, which informs the passions of conflict, the instincts of nutrition, and reproduction, is not always the language of propriety, grammatical correctness and logical consistency. It is the language, however, with which the nervous system in moments of tension and relaxation lives and makes a part of itself. The sources of unconventional language lie deep and its power is irresistible as a force of nature.

Conventional speech is for consideration, for measured distance. Slang is for spontaneity and intense emotional intimacy.

It is largely the language of expression rather than that of communication. The conventional is for distance; it holds from group to group, from generation to generation, from age to age. It tends toward permanence of form. The unconventional is for depth of appeal; it is individual and intimate. It is also unstable and temporary. But however fitful, irregular, and protean it may be, the impulses that inform it are permanent. As there always has been so there always will be an unconventional language.

While some terms last, it exists in a state of ever-evolving fluidity; meanwhile its fundamental themes, as will be seen, remain very much the same. Its immediacy will invariably render its dictionaries obsolete other than for historical references even as they are first published. The force of nature, however, continues unabated.

A 'counter-language'

If slang has a unifying essence, and here it is undoubtedly an abstract one, though rarely expressed as such in its own vocabulary, it is opposition. The undermining of the standard. Slang is too easily dismissed as 'dirty words' but its central role is not obscenity but subversion. This is not, of course, political subversion, but a subversion of the English language itself. This may not seem immediately apparent in the context, for instance, of the obscene terms with which it is so automatically associated, but even there it is so. Slang invariably acts against, and in the case of 'dirty words' it is setting itself in opposition to, 'clean' ones. But such terms are only a small group of the wider lexis. Considered as a whole the slang lexis offers a voice to the outsider, be they professionals, i.e. criminals, or set there by society, i.e. the poor or the young. Like the 'counter-culture' of the 1960s, it represents, in its entirety, a form of 'counter-language'. The standard for this epitome of the non-standard is to say 'no'.

That achieved, one may suggest that it subverts the givens of the world that English informs. Slang may abound in seeming neologisms, but the bulk of its vocabulary is based on the recycling of terms that are well established in standard use. Slang takes them over, turns and twists them, and offers them up in new combinations and senses. As for its speakers, this rejection of standard language and adoption of its 'counter' allows a means of self-definition that places him or her beyond the 'standard' world. The phenomenon of code-switching—adopting one's speech patterns to a given environment, changing for instance between home/school/friends—shows that one cannot (other than in closed worlds such as prison) exist purely in 'slang world'. Just as for the majority some form of 'uniform' must be donned to enter work, so must slang be changed for something less uncompromising to enter the 'real' world. Those who criticize slang's use today tend to emphasize the potential pitfalls of rejecting such practical fluidity, and position themselves as linguistic social workers rather than language purists, but few slang users ignore code-switching.

Secrecy

> I tells Bet to be on the wido, for a swell was sweet on me for a tail; officed Bet, she tumbled to the fake, and stalled off to the dossery. I take the swell to the tape shop, took our daffies, officed Lumming Ned and Scrapping George; they stalled off to the dossery, where I take my green 'un; pinches his skin and ticker, darks the lumber, and planted Flabby Bet on him; she eased him of his fawney, tipped him the glue, officed her cullies, they pasted his nibs, and scarpered rumbo.

> *The Swell's Night Guide* (1846)

No one would think that this passage, recounting the robbery of a hapless countryman lured into a tavern, tricked by a whore, and beaten by her male confederates, was taken down verbatim. (That said, its compiler must have been skilled in the lexis he was using: its representation is quite feasible.) It is culled from a far longer narrative in cant, appended to one of the many gentleman's guides to louche, mid-19th-century London; its ostensible purpose, and one that justified the compilation of many similar confections: to arm the unwary against villainy. Whether the average 'green 'un' made head or tail of the language, let alone committed enough to memory to translate the mutterings around him, is unlikely. But like its many equivalents, both prior and post, the impenetrability of the words displayed represents the whole purpose of a slang vocabulary: keeping things dark, other than for a small band of privileged initiates. Criminal dialogue, springing for most hearers from a wholly unknown world, is exceptionally dense, but it is far from exceptional in its purpose. Slang, at least at its birth, is not intended to be for public consumption.

According to recent research, some 52 per cent of terms used in the English language exist outside the dictionaries. There is, claim the experts, what might be termed a 'dark lexis', the equivalent of the 'dark net', that hidden, even clandestine Internet that can be found 'beneath' the one the majority access, mimicking in its invisibility that submerged sixth-sevenths of our dwindling icebergs. This figure, which is based on comparing the contents of electronic corpora with those of mainstream printed dictionaries, may seem high, and it is possible that a wider sweep of specialist glossaries, whether printed or on-line, might reduce it somewhat, but it has to remain substantial. Slang, en-dictionaried or not, is a representative of that dark lexis.

We have rejected the etymology of *secret lang*uage, but one cannot understate the role of conscious secrecy in the formation and use of slang. The French lexicologist Albert Niceforo, writing in *La Genie de l'argot* in 1912, suggested that:

> Every group, every association however small, from the single couple to the largest group, which feels the need of defense in the environment where it lives, creates an argot for the purpose of concealing its thought; second, the more the necessity of defense and the severity of the struggle are accentuated the more does argot complete and extend itself.

In theory and in practice slang does indeed grasp at invisibility. This was intentional. The word itself, defying easy origins, sets the pattern. Hotten, writing in 1859 when 'civilian' slang had long since invaded the vocabulary, proclaimed his belief that slang had Romani roots. He was wrong—and George Borrow had already unpicked the Gypsies' 'secret language' Romani in *Lavengro* (1851) and *The Romany Rye* (1857)—but the lexis he collected has never given up its meaning without a struggle. Thus was the intention of its users. If, as critics attest, they seem unable to deal with standard speech, what one is meeting is not ignorance but a conscious decision to bypass or at least blur comprehension. As ever one must look back, to a world in which cant, a deliberately concocted amalgam of terms, gave its users a form of communication that successfully baffled hearers, specifically those in authority. Cant would continue on these lines, and if it gradually became more accessible, then its intention remained the same. It is harder now to argue that slang is a secret language, as was once undoubtedly true. Even when our communications are not being actively spied upon, the concept of privacy has become something of an illusion. Nonetheless the need for a level of perceived secrecy remains: when a slang word is coined it may well enjoy a period, however brief, of 'invisibility'. Thus the need for the increasing lists of synonyms. It is not simply for fun. Once a term has become 'revealed' then the immediate need is for re-coinage. It may be ephemeral (though much slang is remarkably long-lived), but as will be seen in Chapter 4 the imagery behind it, the great recurrent themes of the lexis remain the same.

'Slang' or local use

Beyond any detailed analysis, 'slang' has always been a useful grab-bag, a go-to repository of non-standard terms. This, inevitably, has led to errors in categorization, especially from those observing rather than using the local language. Anything that appears 'odd' or even 'picturesque' tends to be lumped together as 'slang'. Whether it is becoming apparent that lexicographers have been either lazy or ignorant, or that reclaiming one's language is part of a wider re-emergence of nationalist consciousness, there has of late been a movement to counter this.

The Australian lexicologist Sidney Baker, writing in 1945, titled his book-length study *The Australian Language*, but much of his word lists would reappear in slang dictionaries, including his own. The authoritative *Australian National Dictionary* (1988) has abandoned the label. Nor does it use 'colloquial', though surely much of such terminology is, and this seems to recall the *OED*'s original definition, which defines slang in term of colloquial language. A similar reticence is found in a major Caribbean dictionary, where one finds divisions into 'Formal', 'Informal', and 'Anti-Formal', but again no 'slang'. Yet there exist, on- and off-line, many volumes entitled 'Australian Slang' and one can find similar publications devoted to the West Indies. Scots has suffered a similar treatment. The knee-jerk response to non-standard uses in the work of Walter Scott, or more recently Irvine Welsh, has been to assume them to be slang. Closer analysis makes clear that this is often not the case, and that the terms are either nativisms or even dialect. This is not to exclude genuine uses of slang, typically in Welsh, some of whose texts almost demand the reader to act also as translator, but much is surely local.

Chapter 4
The words of slang: themes and development

Slang's thematic range is not wide, though its synonymy runs very deep, and as noted one can see the same ideas recurring from classical Greek and Latin onwards. Its conceptual 'waterfront' is narrow—it has almost no time, for instance, for abstractions or philosophizing—but very dense. The very narrowness of this 'waterfront' is the best testament to its utility. Stripped down, modern, cutting edge—at whatever time, that is, that it has reflected the currently 'modern' and whatever edge has been at that moment 'cutting' (Figure 4).

The endurance of this synonymity (which critics have termed 'over-lexicalization'—i.e. too many words for the same thing) and its fundamental role within slang offers rival interpretations: on the one hand one can see it as a means of avoiding the real world (as represented by standard English) by conjuring up an infinity of parallel terms. On the other it suggests a better means, by offering up so many possible descriptions, of burrowing deeper inside it.

The lack of abstracts, suggests Frank Sechrist, stems from slang's rootedness in the solid world. It is happiest, most confident with the tangible:

> It keeps oriented to the sense of touch, contact, pressure, preferring
> a language material which is ultimately verifiable by the most

Once Try, You'll come again
To HARRIS'S

(Established upwards of 20 years)

SLAP UP TOG, AND OUT AND OUT
KICKSIES BUILDER,

1, BACK HILL, HATTON GARDEN,
AND
33, WESTON STREET, SOMERS TOWN.

MR. H. nabs the chance of putting his customers awake, that he has just made his escape from Russia, not forgetting to clap his mawleys upon some of the right sort of Ducks to make single and double-backed Slops for gentlemen in black, when on his return home he was stunned to find one of the top manufacturers of Manchester had cut his lucky, and stepped off to the Swan Stream, leaving behind him a valuable Stock of Moleskins, Cords, Velveteens, Plushes, Swans Downs, &c. and having some ready in his kick—grabbed the chance—stepped home with the swag—and is now safely landed at his crib. He can turn out Toggery of every description very slap up, at the following low prices for

READY GILT—TICK BEING NO GO.

Upper Benjamins built on a downy plan, a monarch to half a finnuff. Slap up Velveteen Togs, lined with the same, 1 pound, 1 quarter and a peg. Moleskin ditto, any color, lined with the same, 1 couter.—A pair of Kerseymere Kicksies, any color, built very slap-up, with the artful dodge, a canary. Pair of stout cord ditto, built in the "Melton Mowbray" style, half a sov. Pair of Broad Cord ditto, made very saucy, 9 bob and a kick. Pair of Moleskin, all colors, built hanky-spanky, with double fakement down the side, and artful buttons at bottom, half a monarch. Pair of stout ditto, built very serious, 9 times. Pair of out and out fancy sleeve Kicksies, cut to drop down on the trotters, 2 bulls. Waist Togs, cut long, with moleskin back and sleeves, 10 peg. Blue Cloth ditto, cut slap, 14 peg. Mud Pipes, Knee Caps, and Trotter Cases, built very low.

A decent allowance made to Seedy Swells, Tea Kettle Purgers, Head Robbers, and Flunkeys out of Collar. N.B. Gentlemen finding their own Broady can be accommodated.

☞ *Observe the Address!*

1, Back Hill, Hatton Garden, and 33, Weston Street, Somers Town.

D

The words of slang

4. This purported advertisement for Harris's 'Slap Up Togs', written in both standard English and contemporary slang, appeared as an appendix to Ducange Anglicus' slang dictionary *The Vulgar Tongue* (1857).

realistic sense. It tends to relate itself to the immediate surroundings and to change with the changing conditions of the time. It is the language of the here and the now. It is limited to the concrete, ridicules the abstract and remote. In some of its forms, it affects a lack of orientation, is far-fetched, extravagant, because it is so sure of its realities. It has so certain a step that it plays with the objects of its thought.... Its affectations, euphemisms, and contradictions seem to rise from a secure perception of reality. It is the language of reality such as common sense conceives it.

That does not exclude nuance. Slang may be restricted in its themes, but its very nature—the whole *raison d'être* is, after all, informality—can make it hard to know just what the user means. It is loose talk in its most literal sense: it cavorts, plays, stumbles about. It does not, at times, make sense and this is not always the product of conscious secrecy. But nor is this a matter of vocabulary, it is one of speech.

If the individual words and phrases that make up the vocabulary may be dismissed as 'ephemeral'—and given the longevity of many slang terms that is a far from accurate dismissal—the persistence of these themes ensures that slang lasts. The imagery does not vanish; it is not short-term. It reflects the way that we think of certain topics. One might call it stereotyping, since it is often in stereotypes that slang deals, but could a better synonym be psychological 'shorthand'?

Man-made language

That psychology, it should be noted, is almost invariably male. The 'male gaze' in linguistic form. That slang is sexist is a given; it is also racist, nationalist, ageist, sizeist, and variously -phobic. Sex, its main preoccupation other than crime and drink, is unlikely to escape its overriding cruelties. However valid, feminist complaints against standard English as a 'man-made' language pale against any assessment of slang's lexis. If one looks, for instance, at the

1,750 terms that focus on heterosexual sexual intercourse, perhaps fifty at most take a woman's point of view (and that almost always passive). If one looks at the genitals, then the penis rejoices in its role as a gun, knife, club, dagger, and so on: a toy for the boys, one might suggest. The vagina, unsurprisingly, is all *dentata* and dark, threatening alleyways though, in fairness, it can, especially at slang's more literary end, be the site of masculine delight. The lexis permits twenty terms for the clitoris but female pleasure is not considered and lesbians are seen essentially as 'freaks'. Procreation, of course, plays no part.

The id made word

Psychology seems some way from slang, with its obsession with the concrete, but it is there. With its vulgarity, its crudity, its impudence, its irrepressible *loudness* it offers a vocabulary and a voice to all our negatives. Our inner realities: lusts, fears, hatreds, self-indulgences. It subscribes to nothing but itself—no belief systems, no true believers, no faith, no religion, no politics, no party. It is, for Freudians, the linguistic id.

The id, as laid out in the *New Introductory Lectures on Psychoanalysis* of 1933:

> is the dark, inaccessible part of our personality,...most of this is of a
> negative character....We all approach the id with analogies: we call
> it a chaos, a cauldron full of seething excitations...It is filled with
> energy reaching it from the instincts, but it has no organization,
> produces no collective will, but only a striving to bring about the
> satisfaction of the instinctual needs subject to the observance of the
> pleasure principle.

If so, then slang is first and foremost less a language phenomenon than a psychological one: it seems visceral, an innate, inescapable need. Standard English certainly addresses such negatives, but never in such unfettered, luxurious indulgence.

The city: slang's ultimate source

SLANG represents that evanescent, vulgar language, ever changing
with fashion and taste, ... spoken by persons in every grade of life,
rich and poor, honest and dishonest ... Slang is indulged in from a
desire to appear familiar with life, gaiety, town-humour and with
the transient nick names and street jokes of the day.... SLANG is the
language of street humour, of fast, high and low life ... Slang is as
old as speech and the congregating together of people in cities. It is
the result of crowding, and excitement, and artificial life.

John Camden Hotten, Introduction to
The Slang Dictionary (1859 et seq.)

Slang is urban. The countryside maintains region-based dialects,
albeit somewhat eroded and certainly altered since the industrial
revolution began moving former peasants off the farm into the
factory. Nor, though its lexicographers have yet to take full note,
does the slang of every city mimic that of the metropolis. And
slang's countryside origins are there: my own database offers nearly
1,000 slang etymologies that depend on local dialects, probably
imported by that same industrial revolution, bringing village
localisms into the crowded industrial streets. Still, the city provides
slang's consistent home. The history of slang is also the history of
the urbanization of modern life as reflected in this influential subset
of the language. One may suggest a simple rule: no city, no slang.

This is never more apparent than in the story of American slang.
Now so seemingly omnipotent and based in the worldwide
dissemination of American popular culture, its story is short,
much shorter than that of America itself. Not until the late
19th century, and the growth of major cities, do native slang
coinages, with a strong presence of imported regionalisms, start
fully to develop. Prior to that the story is largely limited to New
York, and that mainly to its criminal underworld. This is equally
true of African-American slang, now so vital, but effectively

invisible—assuming that it existed—until the former plantation workers began to make their move northwards. The 'nigger minstrel' show, from its birth around 1830 among the 19th century's most popular entertainments on either side of the Atlantic, and almost invariably presented by white men in blackface, offers no slang, merely grotesque misrepresentations of black speech.

Slang has always been subject to negative value judgments: 'sub-standard', 'low', 'vulgar', 'unauthorized'. These live in the ears of the critic, but the *mot juste* for these essentially urban communications is that which itself emerges from contemporary slang: *street*. Street as noun, more recently street as adjective. The gutter language, a coinage that, as first recorded by the *OED* in 1892, comes coupled with the word 'slang'. The vulgar tongue.

A slang taxonomy

Compared with the seemingly endless labours committed to the lexicography of standard English (the original *OED* took nearly fifty years, the current revision stretches out towards an unstated future and like its predecessor will surely demand new researches once that task is 'finished') assembling the slang dictionary is usually simple. Not simply that there are fewer slang terms than standard ones (around 130,000 as against the 600,000 currently offered by the on-line *OED*, of which in turn just 7,766 are labelled 'slang') but there is so much more repetition. Whether or not slang qualifies as a language or is, as suggested, just a very wide-ranging collection of synonyms, certain themes predominate and with them certain definitions. It may not deal with every aspect of life, but what it does consider, it tackles in depth. Slang is insatiable in its search for reinvention, even if what it invents is as often as not more of the same. The *OED* offers 382 terms for drunk, and of these almost exactly half (188) are labelled as slang. Slang's full synonymy for 'drunk' offers well over 2,000 and in common with those of slang's other 'best-sellers' that list is not finite.

As a lexicographer of slang and thus writer of definitions I have written the two words 'the penis' 1,450 times, 'the vagina' 1,400, and 'sexual intercourse', by which I mean the heterosexual variety, 1,740. Oral and anal sex make a substantial showing. I have added such occupational or geographical labels as 'Und.' for 'Underworld' or 'Aus.' for 'Australia' even more frequently. I allow for detail; it is necessary to be precise: sometimes it is a large penis, sometimes a small one, sometimes flaccid, sometimes erect. Sometimes a penis is just a penis. The same, with local variations, goes for the vagina and for intercourse.

'The chief stimuli of slang,' stated J. Y. P. Greig, otherwise known for his work on David Hume, here writing in the *Edinburgh Review* in 1938, 'are sex, money and intoxicating liquor.' The last century or so has added the language of recreational drugs, just one more intoxicant, even if it has drawn the short straw as regards legality, but very little has changed. Drawing again on my own work, an outline taxonomy of my slang database, which runs to approximately 130,000 words and phrases over a period of 500 years and covering all English-language slang, offers the following (rough) statistics:

> Crime and Criminals 5012; Drink, Drinks, Drinking and Drunks 4589; Drugs 3976; Economics (Money / Rich / Poor) 3342; Women (almost invariably considered negatively or at best sexually) 2968; Fools and Foolish 2403; Men (of various descriptions, not invariably, but often self-aggrandizing) 2183; Sexual Intercourse 1740; Penis: 1451; Vagina 1400; Homosexuals/-ity 1238; Prostitute/-ion 1185; Policeman / Policing 1034; Masturbate/-ion 945; Die, Death, Dead 831; Beat or Hit 728; Mad 776; Anus or Buttocks 634; Terms of Racial or National abuse: 570 (+ derivations = *c*.1000); Defecate/-ion & Urinate/-ion 540; Kill or Murder 521; Promiscuous / Promiscuity 347; Female Breast 303; Unattractive 279; Nonsense 271; Fat 247; Oral Sex 240; Vomiting 219; Anal Sex 180, STDs 65.

What we will not find are caring, sharing, compassion, and the like. Perhaps such abstracts require a degree of distance, of thought that eludes slang's worldview. But again, it is the id, not the super-ego.

The development of the slang vocabulary

These themes, in the proportions roughly suggested by the taxonomy, persist throughout slang's history. Like standard English the size of the lexis expands and dictionaries grow ever larger, but unlike it, slang does not move outside its long-established, self-imposed boundaries. Its geographical range may increase—first Australian slang is added to the list, then the creations of post-colonial America, then the slang lexes of other countries such as New Zealand, South Africa, or those islands of the West Indies where English is the first language—but its preoccupations are very static for so intrinsically dynamic a lexis. There emerge and briefly flourish certain trending terms, such as *quoz, flare up*, and others recorded by Charles Mackay in his *Memoirs of Extraordinary Popular Delusions* (1841), but having burnt brightly they soon flame out. There are certain anecdotally driven creations, and rhyming slang may offer some brief fame to otherwise secondary figures, but slang is above all a product, however ludic and reoriented, of the standard vocabulary.

Slang, at least figuratively, remains the language of that true-and-trusted youthful triumvirate: drugs, sex, and rock 'n' roll. Such was slang at the beginning; such, one may safely assert, it will be in the future. It has proclaimed its turf, and like a street gang that dominates its own few blocks and has no wish to venture further is satisfied to maintain its boundaries.

It is true that certain technologies, typically the mobile phone, encourage certain new terminologies, notably the abbreviations and acronyms that have proved so useful for texting, but these are ephemeral, the product of that technology (Figure 5). As a report commissioned by the mobile phone makers Samsung noted in May 2015 the original batch of Internet slangisms—typically

5. Textspeak keyboard: no such keyboard exists, but the possibility is there, and the texting abbreviations it includes reflect today's widespread use of such terms.

abbreviations such as LOL—is being replaced by terms, generated by social media, that are not dictated by the limits of a tiny screen. In time, it suggested, the emoji or emoticon may even provide the primary form of correspondence.

We must work with what we have. It is pleasing to ponder Hotten's claims as regards the slangs of the pre-classical world, but we have few examples and, if there were non-standard words, they are not therefore 'slang'. The deficiency continues well into early modernity. Words that, in time, would qualify as slang can be found as early as 1000, when in his glossary of Latin to Anglo-Saxon Abbot Aelfric includes *ars* (for *podex*; the buttocks) and *beallucas*, i.e. bollocks (for *testiculae*, the testicles). The word *cunt*, thereafter so taboo that it would never attain standard English, can be found in a 13th-century street name (*Gropecuntlane*, noted in several cities, presumably in the 'red light' area) and Lanfranc's *Cirurgerie*, a medical treatise of *c.*1400. Slang's staples begin to emerge in Chaucer's *Canterbury Tales*, *c.*1387, notably in the vulgarities of the Reeve's and the Miller's tales. Among them is sex: *swive* (to have sexual intercourse), *prick* (to enter a woman), *belle-chose*, *quaint*, and *quoniam* (the vagina; all euphemisms, the latter pair playing on *cunt*), *gay* (of a woman, leading an immoral life or working as a prostitute), *hot* (sexually aroused and/or available), and *loteby* (a mistress). There is defecation: *arse*, *tail* (the anus or buttocks), and *hole* (the anus), *gong* (a privy) and *jordan* (a chamberpot), *fart* and *piss* (both found as nouns and verbs). There are oaths: *Christ! cock* (euphemizing God), *for Christ's sake! Gad* (as in *Gad's precious* and *Gad's bones*), and *nails!* which referred to 'god's nails', i.e. those of the crucifixion. There is, inevitably, drink: *totty* (drunk) and *wet one's whistle*, to take a drink. William Langland also offers a small 'slang' lexis in his religious allegory *Piers Plowman* (1367 and 1386) and adds more themes: women: *bitch*; the fool or madman: *buzzard*, *daffy*, and *lubber*; and the police: *catchpole*. The era also offers another of slang's leading players, the whore: *cat*, *hackney*, *ramp*, and a *tickle-tail*. These are samples, but the total remains small.

What might become slang, in a world where the discussion of certain topics fell increasingly beyond the bounds of polite discourse, was, nonetheless, not yet slang. However important to posterity, Chaucer, Langland, and a few others are but drops in the ocean and it is possible that the 'non-standard' vocabulary was far more widespread than has been recorded—an already substantial city such as London presumably had a working class and they in turn would not have invariably used the language of the elite—but a marginal language used by marginal people came last in a world where print was still a novelty, and confined its products largely to culturally and socially 'important' matters.

The canting crew

Our knowledge of slang, especially in its earliest days, is over-dependent on its lexicography (see Chapter 7). This begins in the 16th century when Robert Copland's *Hye Waye to the Spital House*

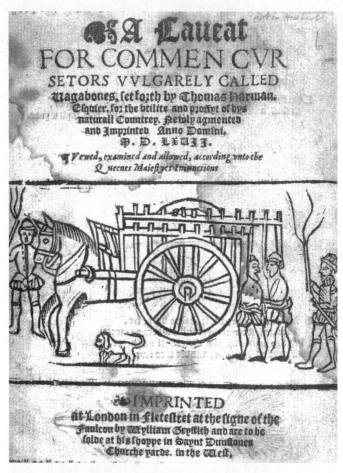

A Caueat

FOR COMMEN CVR

SETORS VVLGARELY CALLED

Uagabones, set forth by Thomas Harman.
Esquier, for the vtilite and profyt of hys
naturall Countrey. Newly agmented
and Imprinted Anno Domini.
M. D. LXVII.

¶ Vewed, examined and allowed, according vnto the
Queenes Maiestyes iniunctions

IMPRINTED
at London in Fleetestret at the signe of the
Faulcon by Wylliam Gryffith and are to be
solde at his shoppe in Saynt Dunstones
Churche yarde. in the West,

6. The frontispiece of Thomas Harman's *Caveat for Common
Cursetors* (*c.*1566). Harman's guide to criminal beggars and con-men
and their 'canting' vocabulary offers both lexical and sociological
information and a good deal of 'true crime' titillation.

(*c.*1535) presents England's initial contribution to a Europe-wide production of 'beggar-books', which offered both the 'job descriptions' and vocabularies (with 'translations' and artificially confected specimen 'conversations') of contemporary criminal beggars, known in England as 'the canting crew' and speaking a criminal jargon known as *cant*. Such pamphlets—Copland was succeeded by John Awdeley's *Fraternity of Vagabonds* (*c.*1561) and Thomas Harman's *Caveat for Common Cursetors* (*c.*1566) (Figure 6)—were part of a general movement towards the codifying and glossarizing of niche occupations, e.g. archery and cooking. The world of criminals, the lists of whose jargon focused less on violence but on confidence trickery and prostitution, was another, if perhaps the 'sexiest' with its mix of supposedly privileged information and legitimized voyeurism.

Given cant's true role as a jargon specific to a time and place, few of these 16th-century terms still exist, although Copland's inclusion of *booze*, albeit as *bouse*, for drink and Harman's of *duds* for clothes established a pair of slang's hoariest veterans. But nothing else survives, even if Joyce appropriated chunks of Harman for *Ulysses* and more recently certain 'medieval' computer games have rediscovered the vocabulary to give words to their villains. In 2009, suggesting a more traditional use, the *Daily Mail* headed a story: 'Convicts use ye olde Elizabethan slang to smuggle drugs past guards into prison', but disappointingly such terms as were provided owed more to Shelta, the tinkers' jargon, than to cant. The elaborate lists that named each rank of the criminal hierarchy and which expanded as one canting dictionary followed another, all the way to the late 18th century, have vanished, even if their trickster specialities can be seen on our modern streets (and were prefigured in an Arabic beggars' glossary of *c.*950 CE).

The display of cant soon passed from beggar books to more creative use, typically in the work of Jacobean playwrights such as Thomas Dekker, Thomas Middleton, or Ben Jonson. Its appearance might be somewhat artificial—a few scenes spoken in such dense jargon that it seemed little more than a glossary en-dramatized, then back to standard speech—but it showed the playwright's insider skills and offered the public a new frisson. Shakespeare, from whom one may glean examples of 500 non-standard terms and who may thus be seen as a pioneer of moving slang beyond the purely criminal milieu, is the contemporary exception: his plays resound with villainy, but other perhaps than in *The Winter's Tale*'s Autolycus, they sidestep beggary and aim at greater malfeasances. Dekker, like his near contemporary Robert Greene whose own plays eschewed criminal vagabonds but who saw the profits in acquainting readers with the 'coney-catching', i.e. confidence trickster, underworld that he claimed to know at first hand, also wrote his own canting pamphlets. More discursive than the beggar books they still combined anecdote with lexis and underpinned the text with a more or less sincere moralizing.

The tradition of canting glossaries, soon expanded into full-scale dictionaries, would persist, even if there was little in-depth attempt to penetrate the changing state of current criminality and every successive lexis made sure to include the same, long defunct core of terms at its heart. Such lexica in turn would provide food for a variety of creative individuals. First playwrights, then criminals themselves, whose 'true confessions' or 'dying speeches' would be peddled almost before their corpse had stopped twitching on Tyburn's notorious Triple Tree, that celebrated gallows (standing near modern London's Marble Arch) that would inspire some eighty slang nicknames. Creative canting was not, however, inevitable. Gay's *Beggar's Opera*, a vast theatrical hit in 1728, is almost slang-free, for all that it showcased low life and has a fence as its villain and as its hero the highwayman Macheath.

By the 19th century the borrowings had become more sophisticated. Harrison Ainsworth confessed to having extracted all his terms from a dictionary of 1819, and used it to add fake, if feasible 18th-century songs to his tales of Jack Shepherd and other villain-heroes. The 'Newgate novelists' of the 1830s, such as Bulwer-Lytton, he of 'it was a dark and stormy night...', stole unashamedly, adding atmosphere and seeming accuracy to their blood-and-thunder melodramas. Dickens fills *Oliver Twist* with the criminal lexis although it was noted that Oliver himself, against all likelihood, spoke purest standard. So too does the street prostitute Nancy, a *scrub* in contemporary slang but thus rendered 'pure' in Dickensian terms, in complete contradiction to what might have been reality. Down the market the penny-dreadfuls and shilling shockers took their share. And if the country-house murders of detective fiction's mid-20th century 'golden age' chose to withdraw their skirts from such contamination, criminal terminology remains a bedrock of *noir* fiction and beyond that film and TV. The works of Dashiell Hammett, Raymond Chandler, W. R. Burnett, and more recently James Ellroy or George Pelecanos, plus hundreds of peers, are dense with all forms of slang, criminal and other. Film naturally abounds with the lexis, whether as purveyed by Warner Bros. in the 1930s and 1940s, Quentin Tarantino fifty years later, or through more recent examples. Though only one, the 1942 comedy *Ball of Fire*, sees it from the lexicographical point of view, following the adventures of a gang of academics as they enter the lower depths, or at least the world of swing and jazz, in aid of their lexicon. Crime, as much as in 1560, continues to fascinate. On television HBO's *The Wire* was perhaps the finest example of a slang-dense script, and many watchers were forced to use subtitles to disentangle the slang terms from what seemed the impenetrable accents of black Baltimore. Understanding what they meant was another problem. The days when a play such as *The Squire of Alsatia* (1688) conveniently provided a small printed list of cant to help playgoers are over, although some mid-20th-century novels still carried a glossary.

The vulgar tongue

The shift of 'slang' dictionaries away from cant and towards today's domination by 'civilian' slang was gradual, but it reflects similarly gradual changes in the spoken use of the counter-language. Despite being titled *A New Dictionary of the Canting Crew*, the work of the otherwise anonymous B.E., published *c.*1698, has been called the first 'slang dictionary': it actually included a substantial number of non-criminal terms. Though some might wait until 1785 when slang's equivalent to Samuel Johnson, the militia captain and antiquary Francis Grose, published the first edition of his *Classical Dictionary of the Vulgar Tongue* and extended the process even further. Grose's title, which for the first time chose to eschew the term 'cant' ('slang' itself would not appear in a dictionary title until 1859), presented non-standard speech, irrespective of origin, as a general 'vulgar tongue', with the term 'vulgar' meaning not so much coarse, as pertaining to the great popular mass. The choice is open, but even though the flow of cant collections continued, these major works showed the way slang was moving.

It would be wrong to suggest that some kind of tsunami of non-standard speech was overwhelming British conversation. Though some contemporaries saw it thus. The early 18th century had seen a movement, pioneered by such as Jonathan Swift, to establish some form of British Academy, and even if he was too intelligent a lexicographer to perform as expected, Johnson was commissioned to write a Dictionary that, like the French equivalent produced by the Académie Française, would set 'correct' language in stone. Nor did slang as such seem to be Swift's only target; he deplored words like *bamboozle*, *phiz*, and *incog*, but also shortcuts such as *tho'* and *couldn't*. Though Swift too enjoyed the devil's lexis, albeit in a somewhat classier version. His *Polite Conversation* (1730) skewers the vocal mannerisms of a gang of gossipy sophisticates in a way that prefigures Nancy Mitford's teasing of her social circle's verbal snobberies in *Noblesse Oblige* (1956).

Grose's introduction shows how he, and doubtless many others, now saw non-standard speech:

> The many…cant expressions that so frequently occur in our
> common conversation and periodical publications, make a work
> of this kind extremely useful, if not absolutely necessary, not
> only to foreigners, but even to natives resident at a distance from
> the metropolis, or who do not mix in the busy world; without
> some such help, they might hunt through all the ordinary
> Dictionaries…in search of the words.

He may call it 'cant', and his dictionary includes a fair selection of
the usual suspects, but this is not the language of the underworld.
It is rather that of 'common conversation', of 'periodicals', of the
'metropolis' and the 'busy world'. It is a language that was by now
in wide use, even if it fell beneath the standards of prescriptive
lexicography. It was also, in its unfettered freedoms, the language
of a true Briton. The French might choose to obsess over 'proper'
and permitted language; Britannia, a true democrat who needed
no revolution, had no time for such foreign tyranny.

It was a view that can be found in slang's next fictional success
story, the sporting journalist Pierce Egan's *Life in London*, better
known by the names of its heroes 'Tom and Jerry'. Framed as a
guide to fashionable, far from invariably respectable London, with
the sophisticated 'Corinthian Tom' leading his country squire
friend Jerry Hawthorn, it was not the first of its type, but far and
away the most successful. *Life in London* echoed earlier vade
mecums to the capital, such as Ned Ward's *London Spy* (1699–1700)
and Tom Brown's *Amusements Serious and Comical* (1700). It
took our heroes, plus their bibulous, green-spectacled friend Bob
Logic 'the Oxonian', on a non-stop tour of London high and low. It
is a book dominated, even dictated by slang (which, as a 'London
language', had played an important role for both Ward and
Brown), and its terms come thick and fast. To be precise Egan
offers not slang but a contemporary variation: *flash*, originated
among criminals but appropriated as a form of linguistic
slumming by the fast-living, dissolute Regency buck and his
sidekicks: fellow aristocrats, racing men honest and otherwise

('blacklegs'), gamblers, bookmakers, prostitutes, prize-fighters, and a random selection of parasitic lowlifes. Egan, whose annals of prize-fighting, the multi-volume *Boxiana*, and other works were shot through with flash, was an unrivalled expert. He laid down a template for Robert Surtees, another devotee of non-standard conversations, and thence, at least as far as Pickwick, for Dickens. In 1823 Egan would go on to offer a revision of Grose, although in a seeming paradox, he expurgated what he saw as the Captain's rougher terms. One that he reprieved was Grose's entry for 'FLASH LINGO' defined in 1785 as 'the canting or slang language'. The identification of slang with speech is the first to appear in a dictionary, but as seen, it would remain for Webster actually to position it as a headword.

The 19th century

The story henceforth might be summed up as quantity rather than quality. Expanded quantity insofar as slang becomes increasingly visible as the 19th century passes, and no change in quality since slang, as noted, may produce regular new crops of synonyms but never really veers from its set paths. No statistics, especially those that have to draw on the vagaries of slang use several centuries ago, can be wholly dependable, but slang's graph is marked by a sustained increase in its vocabulary.

Using my own database (as of January 2015) slang's progress runs thus. It should be noted that these are headwords; the nesting of the material means that many of these contain multiple terms: 14th century: 12 headwords; 15th century: 21; 16th century: 1,140; 17th century: 2,482; 18th century: 3,267; 19th century: 13,270; 20th century–present: 33,693.

It takes time for slang's exposure to come up to speed but once one attains the 19th century the story might simply be titled 'more of the same'. A great deal more. Slang's coinages double between the 16th and 17th centuries, put on a further thousand by 1800, then leap ahead. The 19th century more than doubles the entirety of what has come before and the process has vastly intensified since. (This is obviously helped by the growing appearance of slang from sources beyond the UK.) And while slang undoubtedly becomes more visible, one may still ask whether it was a matter of exposure or of a burst of new coinages. It is hard to discern to what extent slang was lying hidden, awaiting the willingness of writers and journalists and of course lexicographers to publicize it, or whether those same individuals realized that the counter-language was finally something one might exploit. If the publications whence it could be extracted prior to 1800 had numbered a few hundred, by 1900 the figures were potentially in the thousands. Not as many as would exist a century on, when slang seems a part of all but the most formal writing, but certainly something widely recognized and understood. It benefited from an increasingly literate population, and from an expanding marketplace for their pennies. It permeated popular entertainment, notably the lighter end of the stage and the music hall, prior to television the working class's default amusement, home of a variety of 'costermonger' stars (usually but not invariably men) for whom slang was an essential part of their character. It could be found in humorous weeklies like *Punch* or *Fun*, and in sporting journals such as the *Sporting Times*, known from the colour of its stock as 'The Pink 'Un'. It might be used to delineate character in the grim Cockney novels of Arthur Morrison and the amusing ones of William Pett Ridge.

Australia

If there is one qualitative change then it is that Britain's slang was no longer alone. Australia's first ever dictionary of any sort came in the form of a glossary of cant appended to the memoirs of the transportee James Hardy Vaux, published in 1819. It would take some time before any follow-ups, both slang and standard, were published towards the end of the century, but Australia had always been more comfortable with publishing non-standard terms, as for instance in the mid-century sporting magazine *Bell's Life in Sydney*, in which the reader could find dozens of terms that would not appear back in what was known as the *Old Dart* for decades, and by the end of the century a conscious effort was under way to create an autonomous 'Australian' speech that owed nothing to the mother country. Driven by the writers of the fiercely nationalist Sydney *Bulletin* such as Henry Lawson, Edward Dyson, or Andrew 'Banjo' Paterson, the movement either coined or popularized a wide range of homegrown words and phrases. It may be argued that not all such terms are slang, but Australianisms, but it is a tradition that remains and Australian coinage remains among the most vibrant.

The 'New' World

After Australia, America. American slang took some time in the making. There are minor examples to be found from Independence onwards, but even at mid-century the primary input came from the regions, usually in the form of some version of local, quasi-dialect humour. It would all feed the growing slang lexis. There were Yankees, grouped as 'crackerbox philosophers', such as Charles F. Browne ('Artemus Ward'), J. F. Lowell ('Hosea Biglow'), T. C. Haliburton ('Sam Slick'), and Seba Smith ('Major Jack Downing'). While their primary purpose was satirical, their use of colloquialisms, often shading into slang, made them a useful source for lexicographers. Further afield the frontiersmen, typically Davy Crockett, offered their adventures (in Crockett's case via William T. Porter's *Spirit of the Times*, the US equivalent to *Bell's Life in London*); Charles Henry Smith's 'Bill Arp' offered a Southern point of view; the Ohio journalist David R. Locke used 'Petroleum V. Nasby' to comment on politics and was read by Abraham Lincoln. Mortimer Thompson wrote as 'Philander Q. Doesticks'. Female characters included B. P. Shillaber's 'Mrs Partington', whose *Life and Sayings* were published in 1854, and Frances Miriam Witcher's 'Widow Bedott' whose *Papers* appeared in 1856. The last of them, Bill Nye, a real-life

Midwestern postmaster whose career began when a personal letter to the President was reproduced and went, in modern terms, viral, sold hundreds of thousands of copies.

Not all dialects were native: 'the melting pot' was gathering ever more refugees from Europe and their accents proved irresistible. Germans were guyed by Charles G. Leland, who would join Albert Barrère in the writing of *A Dictionary of Slang, Jargon and Cant* (1889–90), in his 'Hans Breitmann' poems and the Irish by Chicago journalist Finley Peter Dunne with 'Mr Dooley'. As for the Jews there was the comedy team of Weber and Fields, the comedy sketches of Joe Hayman whose 'Cohen on the Telephone' (1913) sold one million transcripts, and such dialect-infused characters as 'Potash and Perlmutter', a pair of rag-trade businessmen, created by Montague Glass for a Broadway play (and subsequently a silent movie) in 1913. Even the Marx Brothers began as a dialect act: Groucho was German, Harpo Irish, though only Chico, the Italian, kept it up beyond vaudeville.

In 1859 New York City's chief of police George Washington Matsell produced America's first slang dictionary, the *Vocabulum*, subtitled the 'Rogue's Lexicon'. While a cursory glance suggests this was taken wholesale from Egan's revision of Grose, closer inspection proves otherwise: the local input is far from negligible, perhaps 30 per cent of the headwords, though as a policeman's dictionary and intended to inform his own force, it focuses wholeheartedly on crime.

As it did in the UK, an increasingly literate population, the development of mass printing techniques, notably the rotary press, the flourishing of a literary mass market, typically in the proliferation of the dime novel, and the spread of mass entertainments—typically the slang-filled stage adventures of Mose, the 'Bowery B'hoy'—all accelerated slang's accessibility. America was also less squeamish as regards offering slang to the middle market. Rather than offering a horrified glimpse of the great unwashed slang was presented as entertainment in its own right. The work of George Ade, first with *Fables* and then *More Fables in Slang*, made him fabulously rich. The journalist Helen Green wrote of a Broadway theatrical hotel ('The Maison de Shine') and the con-men, morphine addicts, and vaudeville acts who frequented it. George Vere Hobart published twenty-three books as 'Hugh McHugh', celebrating his character 'John Henry' and mocking his critics in prefaces that paraded his latest phenomenal sales figures. Among the many others were Clarence L. Cullen who wrote two volumes of *Tales of the Ex-Tanks* (i.e. ex-alcoholics), W. J. Kountz with *Billy Baxter's Letters* (1899), 'Billy Burgundy's' *Toothsome Tales Told in Slang* (1902), and Roy McCardell's *Conversations of a Chorus Girl* (1903 and seemingly a predecessor of Anita Loos's *Gentlemen Prefer Blondes*). O. Henry occupies a category of his own, but his urban tales such as *The Four Million* (1906) and *The Voice of the City* (1908) are studded with the language of the street.

There was also a new source of amusement: newspaper comics and cartoons. Slang, suggested Frank Sechrist, was innately cartoonish: now cartoons repaid the compliment. The early 20th-century exemplars were the cartoonist T. A. Dorgan, known as TAD and to whom slang coinages are (mis-)attributed just as one-liners are to Wilde or Dorothy Parker, and Bud Fisher's *A Mutt*, created in the form of a racing tip cartoon in 1907 and who, in 1908, would gain a long-term partner called Jeff.

Last, but hardly least, was sport, or its reporting. London's *Sporting Times* may have used a good deal of slang, but it remained something of a novelty act; and the 'Pink 'Un', for all its popularity in clubland and the subaltern's mess, never gained a vast circulation. American 'sporting scribes' such as Ring Lardner, Charles van Loan, and most famously Damon Runyon, set slang at the heart of their work. It was syndicated around America; it was logical that they pushed it into fiction.

Newspapers

Newspapers have been consistently more willing to acknowledge and more importantly to incorporate slang than other media. This may not include the mainstream press—neither the London *Times* nor New York *Times* would permit such vulgarity—but there are a wide range of papers, and not invariably 'low-toned', which felt themselves far less constrained. The first 'newspapers' to appear in England (still pre-UK) were the rival propagandist news-sheets, usually named *Mercurius*, i.e. 'mercury' and modelled on the *Mercure française*, itself launched in France in 1611, that accompanied the mid-17th-century Civil War. Typical among them was the *Mercurius Fumigosus, or the Smoking Nocturnal* which lasted 1654–5, containing 'many strange Wonders Out of the World in the Moon, the Antipodes, Magy-land, Greenland, Faryland Tenebris, Slavonia and other adjacent parts'. It was published for the 'mis-understanding of all the Mad-Merry-People of Great Bedlam'. The *Fumigosus* and its peers used slang extensively; some 30 per cent of it had not been seen before. By contemporary standards such papers could be quasi-pornographic: *Magy-land* referred to the world of prostitution and appropriated its vocabulary. (The *Antipodes* may also have suggested the 'opposite end', not just of the globe, but of the human body.) The same innovatory role continued: following Egan's Regency publications, such mid-century 'sporting journals' as *Bell's Life in London* paraded their slang vocabularies. At the end of the century London's *Sporting Times* maintained the tradition. In the case of the latter there was even a weekly 'Pome' by the dramatist and social commentator George R. Sims, writing as 'Doss Chiderdoss' (supposedly meaning 'Sleep, Gently Sleep') which was composed entirely in rhyming slang. Meanwhile the *Punch* 'Suggestor-in-Chief' E. J. Milliken created the uber-Cockney ''Arry', whose arriviste adventures were catalogued with much slang and who opined,

As to slang, and strong language, and so on, objections to them is
     all stuff;
What are they but anticipation—to-morrer's swell-slang in the
     rough?
That the nobs prig their patter from ours you may see by their plays
     and their books,
And the lingo that's used by FITZFOODLE's inwented by SNOBKINS or
     SNOOKS.

Slang obviously gravitated towards the subversive and raffish, but
it was not restricted to such sheets. Provincial amateurs might
contribute a column to their local weekly. For instance, in 1852,
an anonymous contributor to Cumbria's *Kendal Mercury* (closed
since 1917) penned a four-part series 'On Cadgers'; it was
illustrated with a detailed glossary of criminal talk that in many
cases was quite new. It does not appear to have appeared
elsewhere first. By the early 1920s America's great syndication
systems ensured that such finds ran far beyond their origins. The
new slang of 1922, seemingly geared to young women and possibly
their own invention, was that of the flapper. A 'flapper dictionary'
was duly created: it made the rounds of every small-town
newsroom in the States.

But small towns remain small. If slang lies in the city, for
19th-century America *the* city was still New York. Non-standard
terms began appearing in its often scurrilous press (referenced
satirically by Dickens in *Martin Chuzzlewit*) of the 1830s, and
the volume only increased. Newspapers, as the American
lexicographers John Bartlett and Maximilian Schele de Vere (and
in time Oxford's James Murray) made clear, were the greatest
source of the non-standard. By 1872 Schele de Vere, in the
instruction to his *Americanisms*, could write:

> The most fertile source of cant and slang…is, beyond doubt, the
> low-toned newspaper, written for the masses, which, instead, of
> being a monitor and an instrument of improvement in the hands of

great men, has become a flatterer of the populace, and a panderer to their lowest vices.

The newspaper remains a primary source not simply of slang but of all language. Whether looking back into the now digitized, searchable files of city or small-town papers, increasingly available on-line, or accessing the contemporary press, newspapers provide an invaluable record. It is unsurprising that they are seen as a foundation stone for the corpora on which modern dictionaries are based.

Modernity

By the 20th century slang could no longer be corralled. We can no longer attempt to itemize its coinages; we are reduced to lists of its popularizers. In January 1934 W. J. Funk, of the dictionary publisher Funk and Wagnall's, offered his list of the 'ten modern Americans who have done most to keep American jargon alive'. They were Sime Silverman, editor of the 'show business bible' *Variety*, the cartoonist 'TAD', the Ziegfeld songwriter Gene Buck, Damon Runyon of 'Guys and Dolls' celebrity, Broadway columnist Walter Winchell, Midwestern humorist George Ade, short story writer Ring Lardner, Gelett Burgess, coiner of 'bromide' and 'blurb', columnist Arthur 'Bugs' Baer, and the iconoclastic critic and lexicographer H. L. Mencken. One can debate the particulars, but the sheer fact of raising slang so high made its position clear.

Playing its new roles—realism, authenticity, manifester of the city and its peoples, voice of the dispossessed, the angry, and the revolutionary, and playing as ever its traditional role as voice of the criminal—it defies easy filing. The literary novel absorbs it, not as enthusiastically as the crime one, but it is there. Among those who have embraced it are John Dos Passos, James T. Farrell, Nelson Algren, John Steinbeck, Saul Bellow, Hubert Selby Jr, James Baldwin, Terry Southern, Robert Stone, Richard Price,

Stephen King, Jonathan Lethem, and Barry Gifford. Not all slang's published employers are stars: checking the frequency of slang by author, among the most cited is the late Seth Morgan. Some have focused on the underside of life, but by no means all. For the writer who desires accuracy, slang is often a given, a necessary ingredient in any depiction of the 'real world'.

African-American slang

If the question of what is genuinely 'slang' and what is in fact local usage touches on the lexes of such countries as Australia or the West Indies, then it bulks far larger when considering what is known as 'African-American slang'. The development, coiners, and users of that slang will be dealt with in Chapter 5, but at this stage it is necessary to question, in this specific context, just what is entailed by 'slang'.

Thanks largely to the worldwide popularity of American popular music, which from its earliest days has been a predominantly black phenomenon (19th-century minstrelsy—in its day almost as internationally popular as jazz or rap—was performed by white men in blackface, but the music proclaimed black origins), the language that is interwoven with successive phases of that music has gained an international audience. The music's current form, hip-hop and rap, brings with it a wide-ranging vocabulary, disseminated through individual contact, in school or college, but more often through lyrics, interviews, the scripts of movies and TV shows, and on-line. It is a truism to suggest that the bulk of modern youth slang finds its roots on America's ghetto streets (a take-up that extends beyond anglophone speakers), but one must also ask: is all of black America's popular speech automatically slang?

The 2010 US census claims some 40 million citizens of African-American descent: they represent 12.3 per cent of the population and are as such the country's second largest ethnic group.

Their forebears came as slaves and it was necessary that the slaves should communicate: to each other and to their masters. Different tribes were unintelligible to each other and slavers were careful to split up tribal groups so as to ensure against rebellious collaboration. None would have been understood by their white masters. What developed was a form of *pidgin* English. It was this pidgin, an Afro-English blend (or in a French colony such as Louisiana Afro-French), that would have been passed on to the slave's children. At this point, in linguistic terms, it becomes a *creole*, defined as a pidgin that has native-born speakers and as such moves from a mongrel status (pidgins are traditionally seen as trade languages used between local sellers and visiting buyers) to being one of the 'proper' languages of the country.

Where this language came from remains problematic. The prevailing opinion of early dialecticians was summarized in 1924 by G. F. Krapp. He saw it as 'a very much simplified English—the kind of English some people employ when they talk to babies'. It was also 'reasonably safe to say that not a single detail of Negro pronunciation or Negro syntax can be proved to have any other than an English origin'. The language changed, he added, moving in the 19th century from 'a grotesque mutilation of the English language' to becoming 'one of the colloquial forms of our many visaged mother tongue'. He refused to acknowledge the least African roots.

Since then the idea of 'mutilation', implicitly racist, has been exploded. But the basis of the language remains debatable: was it, as Afrocentric scholars prefer, based on a mélange of African languages and their grammatical forms or, as Eurocentric dialecticians claim, a form of English picked up from local poor whites, who in turn had imported their dialects from the UK? The near-hysteria aroused by the Ebonics controversy of 1997—when the educational authorities of Oakland, California, determined that Ebonics, literally 'ebony phonics' i.e. Black English, should be considered a separate language and taught as such in schools alongside standard English—proved that a resolution remains problematic. There is simply too much weight beyond the linguistic.

None of which undermines the important fact: Black English, whether named African-American English (AAE), African-American Vernacular English (AAVE), Black English Vernacular (BEV), Vernacular Black English (VBE), or Ebonics, exists: it is the language spoken at least some of the time by America's black population. Its use is class-based—the poorer the speaker the more it is used, often to the virtual exclusion of standard American English—but all classes have the option of code-switching when necessary. In this it resembles slang—and the more vitriolic of Ebonics' opponents dismissed it as no more than slang and as such worthless—in that it is seen as a language of the street, another bottom-up linguistic creation. However, although like any language it includes a slang lexis, it is not 'just slang'. On the most basic level, if slang, as suggested, is not a language—lacking the necessary linguistic rules—then AAVE is, since it has been accepted that whatever its origins—African or European—there is a discernible grammar. It is not simply a lexis of underclass illiteracies, the linguistic version of an impoverished ghetto. The problem for the historian is to distinguish the two.

Chapter 5
The users of slang

Language or lexis, who uses slang? One may posit two groups: the 'primary' users who coin and develop the vocabulary and for whom it works as the basis of their everyday speech, and the 'illustrative' users who employ slang for authenticity. The earliest examples of both groups reach back to early modernity. The wandering criminal beggars who were found all through Europe and who coined their own 'cant' being the coiners; users include the prototype slang collectors, followed quickly by its exploiters: pamphleteers, playwrights, and confectioners of 'last dying speeches' and 'true confessions' who used slang to embellish the 'truth' of what they wrote.

Slang may turn to standard English for the bulk of its vocabulary, but at that point the similarities cease. The acknowledged nature of standard language is that it tends to trickle down. Slang does not: it pushes upwards. If it is the language of the gutter then, looking to impose itself on popular speech, it reaches for the stars. It is, surely, the only register that can claim this topsy-turvy form of creation.

The French critic Daniel Pennac has dismissed slang as 'an underdog's lexicon'. One cannot argue. Or if not invariably the underdog's, since slang has long since moved into wide-ranging use, then the outsider's. Its 'primary' users—the young, the poor, the criminal, the violent, the drug consumers—proclaim themselves. Slang has always been owned, if only symbolically, by those who occupy the margins.

Given its origins as the language of crime, and its continuing association with non-elite social groups, often other than white, this is hardly surprising. Nor is its bad reputation. Slang, it is regularly suggested, represents the user's innate inarticulacy. Not so. The reality is that slang remains in a state of constant reinvention, even if that reinvention is not coming from elite sources. For Frank Sechrist the earliest forms of slang also suggest a more honest form of expression, the antithesis of elite speech, using plain English to offer 'the more informal, unconventional and vital states of mind, the more honest emotions, the deeper feelings of love and hate, of joy and sorrow'.

Theatricality

While slang's concerns make clear its focus on the concrete, there is a less tangible side to its use. The adoption of slang for many may be seen as theatrical, a performance. It is a costume one assumes, a mask which denotes a chosen personality. Even a script, with its innate synonymy demanding the use of many words when 'normally' one would suffice. Slang is a form of linguistic fairground, a carnival with a choice of sideshows.

It is also an open sesame to a variety of social worlds. It provides the user with a necessary key to unlock such gated communities. A linguistic form of secret handshakes, of nods and winks. At the same time, like any form of group code, it can re-lock that same gate behind it, as exclusive as it is inclusive.

Closed worlds

The underworld

The default slang user is the criminal (Figure 7). The first slang lexicography listed his and her jargon, and such glossaries remain a

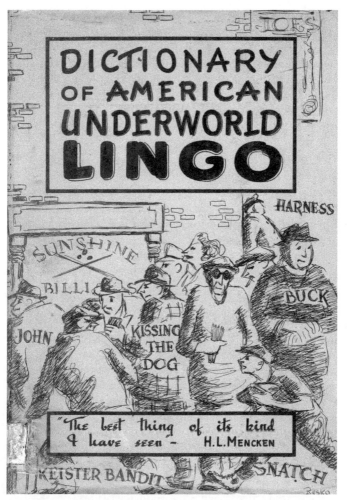

7. The cover of Hyman Goldin's *Dictionary of American Underworld Lingo* (1950). Goldin, a prison chaplain, enlisted as researchers such inmates as 'Bad Bill', 'Bubbles', 'Chop-Chop', 'Dippo', and 'The Colonel'.

staple of the form. Crime demands one of slang's founding principles: secrecy. Its language, however exploited in the modern media, remains a bastion of the art. There is a degree of chicken and egg here: criminals are characterized, especially in fiction, whether in print or on screen, by the language they use. The tradition of embroidering crime-based texts is hardwired into the underworld's fictional representations. Meanwhile, real-life villains look to the screen for 'authentic' terminology.

Prison

The closed world of prison presents a perfect seedbed for the germination of slang. Life is tightly prescribed, there are hierarchies—whether established by officialdom or laid down among the inmates themselves—there is a predictable round of officially circumscribed existence. One may fight the authorities, but one remains in prison. Until one's sentence has been served out (or less frequently in the case of escape) there is nowhere else to go.

Each prison has its own linguistic specialities, often based, as are those of schools and colleges, on specific local references: the name of the prison itself, its buildings, the prison officers, the dinner menu, the internal logistics, such as illicit communication or the smuggling of commodities and those who facilitate such activities, the characteristics, admirable or otherwise, of given types of prisoner. In those countries which maintain it, there is a whole micro-lexis pertaining to the death penalty: the wing that holds the condemned, the room in which it is performed, the means of execution. It is perhaps a subconscious response to this hermetic world that the one group who appear to be overlooked are those who arrive from the free world, the visitors.

Tramps

On one level the hobo/tramp is the descendant of the sturdy beggars of the 16th century. Like them, he is nomadic rather than urban. But the hobo was a traveller rather than a career criminal or con-man, and had a far larger territory to cover. The beggar walked, the hobo rode. The practice, it seems, began when veterans of the US Civil War hopped freight trains to get themselves home. (The UK seems to have pre-dated this, with the publication in 1845 of *Tales of the Trains* by Charles Lever, known as 'Tilbury Tramp', but the relatively tiny UK network could never develop the same mythology: British tramps walked.) The first piece of hobo writing was Bret Harte's 'My Friend the Tramp' (1877): after that hobo-related material became a publishing mainstay, whether as sociological investigation or memoir. Jack London memorialized his experiences; Leon Livingston, self-glorified as 'A-No 1, The Famous Tramp', turned his life into a series of best-sellers and died a rich man on his royalties. The 1930s were glutted with hobo memoirs, usually offering a glossary. Across the Atlantic the London section of George Orwell's *Down and Out in Paris and London* (1933) laid out his experiences among the tramps. By 1931, and published in London by Eric Partridge's Scholartis Press, the lexis justified Godfrey Irwin's full-scale dictionary: *American Tramp and Underworld Slang*.

Drug users

Given what might be seen as the closed world of the drug user, the language of recreational drugs might well be categorized as a jargon. In fact drugs terminology has been appearing in mainstream slang dictionaries for some time. There are simply too many drug users for the lexicographer to pretend that this substantial vocabulary is merely a 'job-specific' subset. It is also hard to isolate drug terms. They impinge on black slang, on youth slang, and on counter-cultural slang. As one set of prohibitions followed another the non-medical use of drugs became a badge of social if not political rebellion, though the Sixties hippies made gestures in that direction. Above all, drug slang takes us back to the justification for the very earliest cant: the need for secrecy.

That slang has gathered around alcohol and tobacco, and especially around alcohol's best-recorded effect: drunkenness

(100 terms already coined by 1600, well over 1,300 in total), is anomalous. Given that they remain legal 'highs' the volume of coinages can be attributed, perhaps, to the substances' role in physical indulgence—always a primary generator of the slang vocabulary—rather than reflecting the need for secrecy that underpins those drugs that have been made illegal. The creation of slang for the other recreational drugs had twin stimuli: the sheer fact of their prohibition and the need for surreptitious consumption and purchase (and thus descriptive language) that accompanied this criminalization, and their stereotyped association with despised or feared minorities (which again lay behind the prohibition).

Looking at the language of drug use it is necessary to differentiate between what truly is jargon and what is more general slang which tends in turn to synonymous names for a given type of drug. The cant specialist David Maurer (1905–81), who had looked at the intricacies of big-time confidence trickery in *The Big Con* (1940; the book upon which the film *The Sting* would be based), published a number of in-depth studies in *American Speech* (e.g. 'Junker Lingo' (1933), 'Argot of the Underworld Narcotic Addict' (1936)) and the book *Narcotics and Narcotics Addiction* (with Victor H. Vogel) in 1954 (revised 1962). These are filled with 'technical' language that would not be found outside the drug users' world, typically laying out the precise names for the equipment used to self-administer narcotics. Such language does not qualify for the general-purpose slang dictionaries.

In addition there are a regular succession of 'trade names' of various drugs as sold on the street: these tend to be too ephemeral for the lexicographers. Nonetheless the field is prolific, and getting on for 2,750 'general-purpose' terms have been in use at one stage or another. Again, their growth is often linked to prohibition. The label 'drugs' is still barely noticeable prior to World War I. The passing of the Harrison Narcotics Act of 1914 multiplied the terminology by a factor of 10; between 1937, when US cannabis use was outlawed in 1937 by the Marijuana Tax Act, and 1960, the dawn of the 'counter-culture', drug terms went up from barely 200 to 730. (In 1936 cannabis offered less than 25 synonyms; 700 have materialized since.) Two thousand more have been coined in the half-century that followed. These are necessarily imprecise figures, but they show the direction of the graph. If the 'war on drugs' has achieved nothing else, then it has constantly replenished the ever expanding store of slang synonyms.

The military

Like those of vagrants and drug users, the world of the military professional is too productive of slang that has crossed over into wider use to be sidelined as mere jargon. There is jargon, a great deal of it—the naming of officers and non-coms and their ranks and occupations, the nicknaming of weaponry and its parts, friendly and otherwise, of regiments, and of course of the enemy—but there is more. Wars end and the troops, at least the fortunate ones (and those less fortunate who have been severely wounded but still survive), come home. And they bring at least a sample of their language with them. It too survives, in their conversations, their memoirs, and, later, in the history books, or certainly those—and there are many such these days—that call on oral testimony. While Hotten's reference to the sources of slang as being 'the congregating together of people...the result of crowding, and excitement, and artificial life' was focused on cities, nowhere could qualify any better for his congregation, crowding, and excitement than does war, especially those protracted engagements such as World War I. If the use of cant in studies and novels of crime confers authenticity to the texts, so too does slang to those of war.

The pattern and nature of war-generated slang continues. A certain number of neologisms arrive home and are absorbed into the language. It is these that are featured in the press and discussed in the journals. But the reality is that brutal circumstances breed, or at least popularize, brutal language.

Perhaps the most celebrated term to emerge from World War II was Norman Mailer's semi-euphemistic *fug*, used in *The Naked and the Dead* (1948), which allegedly elicited Tallulah Bankhead's comment: 'So you're the young man who doesn't know how to spell "fuck"'. Soldiers remain profane. Although profanity is not the whole of their vocabulary. They use the mainstream slang that they have brought with them and terms generated by their respective services. Some terms would be created in-country. They adopted local language, such as those encountered in Korea or Vietnam, and brought some of it home. Each war produced its crop of veterans and the language they had absorbed lasted with them.

The longer the campaign, the more productive of slang it was. World War II, long but lacking the trench warfare of its predecessor, produced less soldier talk. The Falklands and the two Gulf Wars produced little; nor did Bosnia nor the imbroglio in Afghanistan. In an increasingly high-tech battlefield, a world of drones that do their job at the behest of controllers in rooms half a world away, there are no crowded, static trenches for language to develop. Nor is there the leavening of millions of civilian conscripts or volunteers, bringing their own terminology to the front lines and taking a new lexis home. The majority of such slang that is coined remains outside the troops' home countries. 'Embedded', i.e. controlled reporting and an ever-swelling lexis of euphemisms—*collateral damage*, *friendly fire*, *kinetic military action*—have worked against civilians accessing what the soldiers are actually saying. Compared to 1914–18 the river of neologisms has slowed to a trickle.

College and school

If slang is identified with any group today, it is the young. Yet their appropriation of the lexis is relatively recent. The tradition had been that just as the young dressed as junior adults, so did they speak. A working-class youngster would have adopted some slang, but it would have been that of his or her parents. The Artful

Dodger, who is en-slanged even if his pupil Oliver is not, speaks the same cant as do Fagin and Bill Sykes. Alf the 'hooligan' of Clarence Rook's Cockney novel *The Hooligan Nights* (1889) uses the same slangy speech as does his drunken, violent father.

The emergence of youth slang

In 1903, writing in the *Pedagogical Seminary*, a journal of child psychology, Edward Conradi offered a selection of data on 'Children's Interests in Words, Slang, Stories, etc.' The piece dealt with various aspects of the language enjoyed by those under 18, and its centrepiece was a list of some 850 slang terms, gleaned from 295 answers to a questionnaire circulated by high school teachers. These were divided by the gender of those who offered them—'Boys', 'Girls', and 'Sex Not Specified'—and broken down into various subsections: 'Rebuke to Pride', 'Negatives', 'Shock', 'Exaggerations', 'Exclamations', 'Mild Oaths', and a substantial section entitled 'Unclassified' and which included the majority of nouns and verbs. 'Unclassified' themes show terms for 'boasting and loquacity, hypocrisy,... attending to one's own business and not meddling or interfering, names for money, absurdity, neurotic effects of surprise or shock, honesty and lying, getting confused, fine appearance and dress, words for intoxication,... for anger... crudeness or innocent naiveté, love and sentimentality'. A graph was compiled which suggested that slang use peaked between ages 13 and 16.

These categories excluded some of slang's adult themes, but the bulk of terms were certainly slang; and the young people were the age of modern teenagers. And as G. S. Hall noted in 1906, there was a degree of code-switching between classroom and elsewhere: 'Most high school and college youth of both sexes have two distinct styles, that of the classroom which is as unnatural as the etiquette of a royal drawing-room reception or a formal call, and the other, that of their own breezy, free, natural life. This informal "lingua franca" [is] often called "slanguage".' Hall adds that these two 'have no relation to or effect upon each other'; only a 'very few, and these generally husky boys, boldly try to assert their own rude but vigorous vernacular in the field of school requirements'.

Yet this is not 'youth' or 'teen slang'. There is no sense that the lists are designed to set the speakers apart even if the 'husky boys' who used slang in class make them the predecessors of the gang kids of half a century ahead. Nor that the slang was fresh-minted by the young people who used it. There is a certain overlap with contemporary lists of college usage, but the words are those of the era's general slang. Most have been in place for the last decade and many for longer. Certain current linguistic fads are suggested, for instance the twenty-five variations on 'wouldn't that . . .' as used to preface a phrase of shock ('. . . rattle your slats', '. . . fade the stripes on your grand dad's socks', etc.), but there was no generational distinction and the majority of terms are used by all age-groups.

Flappers and alligators

There were, however, some instances of what was effectively teen slang before World War II. The young girls, all shingled hair, rolled stockings, cigarettes, and petting parties, who called themselves flappers (its first use, *c.*1900, was to mean a young or under-age whore; that of the 1920s was far more innocent), underlined their 'rebellious' role by adopting a language of their own. Some could be found already, used in college and high school, and what was not sounded artificial and self-conscious. On either count it was widely publicized.

It is harder to unravel youth slang of the next two decades from that of the mainstream. On the whole it was not analysed, and was usually seen through the prisms of college language or the slang used by 'alligators', fans of jazz and then swing. The language of World War II, with its wide range of military neologisms, slang and others, further crowded out the period's young civilians. The fans who made crooner Frank Sinatra into a superstar were credited with a few terms (e.g. *able Grable* or *whistle bait*, a sexy girl; *glad lad*, an attractive boy; *jive bomber*, a good dancer) and they were duly written up in the press, but none of it lasted and like many such articles, one wonders how much was contrived: whether by the interviewee, keen to please the journalist, or the journalist, keen to amuse the readers.

The teenager

The word *teenage* can be found in 1921 ('in one's teens' has been recorded for 1684), but the modern concept of the teenager as representing a segregated social group is a creation of the 1940s, if not the decade that followed; it was embryonic among the bobby-soxers of the Sinatra era, but it required rock 'n' roll for the teenager proper.

The growing self-segregation of the teenager, carving out their own space in parallel to the adult norms, required a separate language (Figure 8). This was not always especially different: youth would continue to adopt adult slang as well as to create its own. As such much of the vocabulary was not considered worthy of comment. But certain areas generated notice, notably the much analysed 'juvenile delinquent', enjoying and embodying that triple threat of sex, drugs, and rock 'n' roll.

Working-class delinquents aside, slang permeated the language of a succession of what the Sixties would christen 'youth cults' and what the Fifties had already termed 'youth culture' (first noted in 1958). Beats, then beatniks, zoot-suiters and teen gangs, and then hippies each offered a distinct subset of speech. And while slang as ever followed its predictable themes, two strands became increasingly important; the language of recreational drug users and the expanding influence of black slang on white speakers. Like everything the post-war young saw as imitable and alluring it began in America, but the move first to the UK and then beyond soon accelerated. The world-embracing primacy of modern rap,

8. The career of cartoonist T. A. Dorgan, best known as TAD, flourished around 1900–20. Genuine coiner of many slangisms—cat's pajamas, applesauce, drugstore cowboy, dumbell—he became the go-to source for many that he may never have even heard.

the slang of which has moved beyond anglophone speakers, shows the current breadth of the phenomenon.

Class

The use of slang is invariably seen as an indication of the speaker's class. Given slang's origins on the street, there is little upper-class slang. Or little has been recorded: my own database holds 127 terms labelled 'society', and of these more than half come from the 1909 dictionary *Passing English of the Victorian Era* by J. Redding Ware. The working class, criminal or not, have always been and remain slang's leading creators and speakers. The Regency popularity of *flash*, which was certainly spoken cross-class, did not change its origins, which were the underworld, the prize ring, and the race track, and if it took anything from society, then it was only its most raffish end. Its modern equivalents are perhaps what is known as 'mockney', and the adoption by a wide range of classes and ethnicities of the once all-black language of rap. Both suggest another form of linguistic slumming.

Perhaps slang coinages require a grittier reality against which to polish themselves. Even British TV's recent 'reality show' *Made in Chelsea*, set among London's supposedly most gilded youth, could barely manage a dozen terms. There persist, no doubt, a variety of localized slangs within elite schools and colleges on both sides of the Atlantic, but these are jargons, and much reduced from the mid-20th century, when it was possible to publish whole dictionaries of 'Public School' and 'University', i.e. primarily Oxbridge, slang. The most substantial attempts to collect more recent elite slang came in the 1980s: *The Sloane Ranger Handbook* (1982) from the UK and *The Preppie Handbook* (1980) from America. These offered glossaries, albeit limited. There are, inevitably, small vocabularies used among given circles of friends, but in common with any such lists irrespective of class, they do not bulk large enough to be recorded.

At the other end of the social scale slang is the natural province of the poor. They are not restricted to slang, but having been set on society's margins, they are more likely to use non-conventional speech. Slang, with its disdain for idealism and self-improvement, is as unmerciful to poverty as it is to those condemned as stupid or mad or in some way physically inept and its descriptions are no more sympathetic. But the use of slang is not merely a badge of poverty: we have encountered the concept of 'the poor man's poetry', even if the idea is somewhat over-romantic. It is also a badge affixed by middle-class scholars rather than by the impoverished slang-users themselves. Slang's sole term for poetry, used around 1900, is *gruel*, that thin, nutrition-free staple of workhouse misery.

Nor, until the late 19th century, are the poor very much represented in fiction, whether novels or plays, other than as amusing walk-ons, often absurd. Like the Irish, Scots, Welsh, and such foreigners as the French, Dutch, Germans, and Jews, they are easily identified by their heavily accented, and almost certainly mis-transliterated speech. Even Dickens's Wellers, father and son, are still very much of the type. The likes of Sairey Gamp are pure grotesques, with language to match. Not until the 'Cockney novels' of the end of the 19th century are the poor considered as reasonably flesh-and-blood individuals and the (mainly middle-class) authors who ventured into the East End, or the Lower East Side, attempted with varying success to offer fair representation of the way they spoke (see Chapter 6). Social commentators such as Henry Mayhew or James Greenwood offer allegedly verbatim transcripts of their impoverished interviewees, but Mayhew in particular is judged to have embellished reality.

Race: African-Americans

That slang has been and remains unabashedly racist has been noted in Chapter 2. This has in no way affected the continuing rise, for nearly a century, of the unrivalled importance of African-American slang within the anglophone, and latterly worldwide arena. It is fitting that this form of slang, always the city's speech, is sometimes known as *urban*, defined by the current *OED* (2011) as 'of or relating to any of a variety of genres of popular music of a type chiefly associated with black performers... characteristic of or relating to the subculture associated with this type of music. Also: of or relating to black (esp. African-American) popular or youth culture generally.'

The dominant form of current slang is that popularized, primarily through rap music, by African-American artists and, to a lesser extent, by their UK equivalents, whose style is known as *grime* and who have helped evolve a contemporary British slang, known as Multi-Ethnic or Multicultural London English (MLE), a blend of Jamaican patois, US rap terms, Cockney localisms, and pure invention. As with criminals, the use of slang by these groups automatically brands it a problematic lexis.

While far from every slang speaker is in fact black, many people equate black speech with slang. As shown in the arguments over Ebonics, this remains debatable, and bitterly so, but just as black individuals, mainly via music, have had a substantial influence on popular culture for a century, so too has black slang played an increasing role. Through the influence of rap music and the black-coined slang that permeates its lyrics, slang is one more aspect of black culture that has moved to centre stage for young people, whatever their own colour or class.

This lexis draws on several roots: jazz and 'jive talk', the blues and its lyrics, the prison poems known as 'toasts', and the young people's games of ritualized insult, the 'dozens'. Rap, with its rhymes and rhythms, its misogyny and its obsession with sexual conquest, its glorification of violence, its parading of male prowess and the aggregation of material goods, its retailing of stories of confrontations with a white power structure, draws on all.

Jazz/jive talk

The world of jazz, a word coined in the musical context in 1913, soon generated its own vocabulary. As is all slang, but intensified by its black origins, the language of jazz, also known as *jive talk*, was seen as consciously oppositional. It owned to a mongrel lexis, typified by the critic H. L. Mencken in 1948 as 'an amalgam of Negro-slang from Harlem and the argots of drug addicts and the pettier sort of criminals, with occasional additions from the Broadway gossip columns and the high school campus'. The jazz lexicographer Robert Gold sees 'a people in rebellion against a dominant majority, but forced to rebel secretly, to sublimate, as the psychologist would put it—to express themselves culturally through the medium of jazz, and linguistically through a code, a jargon'. It is the classic formulation of a counter-language.

The black journalist Earl Conrad, among others, saw that its importance lay as much in what it did as in what it said, the ideas and energy that it helped release:

> Jive…supplies the answer to the hunger for the unusual, the exotic and the picturesque in speech. It is a medium of escape, a safety valve for people pressed against the wall for centuries, deprived of the advantages of complete social, economic, moral and intellectual freedom. It is an inarticulate protest…a defense mechanism, a method of deriving pleasure from something the uninitiated cannot understand.

Jive talk, like the music and society it reflected, fascinated the lexicographers, academics, and indeed its own users. But what they listed was not uniquely black, nor, as long as musicians and listeners were solely black, did the academics acknowledge its speech. Only when a substantial white audience started turning to jazz, and to an even greater extent to the swing music of the Thirties and Forties—played equally by blacks and whites—did the list-makers turn in its direction. Some of the language was certainly used, and indeed originated by black musicians, but it was not their sole property.

Perhaps its foremost advocate was the musician Milton 'Mezz' Mezzrow, born white and Jewish, but a zealous adopter of black culture. He saw African-American speech as concomitant with the great human movement away from the south. 'It was the first furious babbling of a people who suddenly woke up to find that their death-sentence had been revoked, or at least postponed, and they were stunned and dazzled at first, hardly able to believe it.' The language of southern Negroes had been defensive, a way of hiding from the white world of 'Mr Charlie'. Jive was something else, another code that whites couldn't understand but a code not of subjugation but of resentment, of anger, and of future attack. It was also an assertion of self and the antithesis of the derogatory stereotypes of minstrelsy:

> Once and for all, these smart Northern kids meant to show that they're not the ounce-brained tongue-tied stuttering Sambos of the blackface vaudeville routines, the Lazybones' of the comic strips, the Old Mose's of the Southern plantations. Historically, the hipster's lingo reverses the whole Uncle Tom attitude of the beaten-down Southern Negro.... Deny the Negro the culture of the land? O.K. He'll brew his own culture—on the street corner.

Blues

Jazz was primarily musical, and its slang evolved in parallel. Blues usually offered lyrics and they were dense with slang. As Stephen Calt writes in his dictionary of blues language *Barrelhouse Words*, 'The blues lyric was a snippet of vernacular speech set to song... Recorded blues of the period are so saturated in slang and assorted colloquialisms as to create a peculiar dialect that is only half-intelligible to present-day listeners.' The early blues were raw, both in emotion and vocabulary. Some of the raunchiest were sung by women, notably Louise Bogan. Audiences seemed to relish the sexual references, the singers were happy to provide them. They could be unmediated, but often they resorted to double entendre, carefully sidestepping direct obscenity, knowing that listeners would have no illusions.

Toasts

The toast, which despite a number of arguments over its origins, seems to be linked to the same toast as is given by a drinker, is a form of spoken verse, usually bawdy, almost exclusive to the black community, and primarily encountered in institutions.

The toasting heyday appears to have run from the 1930s to 1970s, and all scholars (collecting at the end of this period) note that the men from whom they gathered the material tended to be at least middle-aged. The majority of them also seemed to be in prison, where the toast was a regular form of entertainment. Although some toasts adapt 'straight' poetry or older cowboy or hobo ballads, the bulk of them relate to 'the Life', the world of the black urban hustler.

Blues and toasts both suggest a degree of 'autobiography' but while the former tend to the general—journeys, jails, the perennial broken heart—the toast claims to recount a specific anecdote, even if its players are far larger and their actions more cartoonishly far-fetched than any real life. They are also set against the city rather than the country that informs many blues. And while the blues, as one would expect, bemoans life's problems, the toasts almost always come in the form of boasts: even stories that end in failure involve a good deal of self-aggrandizement. Some offer a moral, but not until the narrator has shown us that to fall so far he has first been up so high. As opposed to the female dominated blues songs of the 1920s and 1930s, where slang commonly appears in the form of double entendres, the male-delivered and -created toast is always direct. Often grossly so. Toasts employ a wide range of slang, perhaps 50 per cent labelled 'black', and there is no attempt to sidestep those terms considered highly obscene.

'Race novels'

Slang, irrespective of its users, can never abandon its fundamental requirement; the city. The movement to the northern cities, with its gradual creation of semi-segregated black ghettoes, created a new subgenre of black writing, featuring the 'bad man' and his world. White culture was effectively invisible; only life on the ghetto street was portrayed. The creation was not immediate: Richard Wright's Bigger Thomas in *Native Son* (1940), and Ralph Ellison's *Invisible Man* (1953) played the bad man role, but these books and those that imitated them were played out against the hero's struggle against white racism. The writers of the Harlem Renaissance who preceded them were less worried about the bad man, preferring to celebrate the positives in black culture. Zora Neale Hurston, one of the best known, created a 'Story in Slang', but her work tended to range much further, and often beyond the city. It was a third generation, the new writers of the 1960s and 1970s, who showcased street language. Best known were Chester Himes, in his 'Harlem domestic' phase, Donald Goines, and Odie Hawkins. Their plots never left the ghetto and their books can be seen as the toast made book-length prose. As Jerry H. Bryant has put it, 'A cohort of black novelists seems to have deliberately set out to write the "toast" into a new form of fiction. It was a genre not destined for either mainstream popularity or critical acclaim. But it took on the world of the street player with gusto.'

The dozens

'The dozens', otherwise known as *sounding*, *signifying*, *joaning*, the *mama's game*, and most recently and in an abbreviated form *snaps*, is a form of ritualized insult, practised by young and teenage African-Americans. It does not coin slang but uses it, and is seen as a basic way-station on one's necessary progress to linguistic facility. A variety of theories as to its origins have been suggested; the most likely is that it was brought from West Africa with the slaves; such games are still played there, whereas, despite scholarly theorizing, the ritual has not been found in Europe or in white America. Its essence, ritual insult, is paralleled by the 16th century's *flyting*, but while that was the carefully contrived product of poets (it is in William Dunbar's 'Flyting of Dunbar & Kennedy' of 1508 that one finds the first known use of the verb 'fuck'), the dozens are spontaneous and the product of street-level confrontations, either as a substitute for or a prelude to a fight. Flyting also makes no particular target of the mother, the central figure of the dozens.

Gay slang

From one viewpoint 'gay slang' might be seen as a jargon, the property of a single group, but such boundaries are exceptionally fissiparous: is there in fact a single group, and to what extent does the 'gay' lexis overlap with 'straight' language? Given the oppositional status—voluntary or otherwise—of its speakers to the supposedly 'standard', i.e. heterosexual world, it could certainly qualify as a prime example of a literal counter-language. Is there such a thing as 'gayspeak' (a term coined in 1981 in J. W. Chesebro's study *Gayspeak: Gay Male and Lesbian Communication*) with a vocabulary and speech community to match, or is the reality something far more fluid and indefinable, a style? Such questions, and many and far more nuanced others form the fundamentals of modern discussion of the topic. It is beyond the scope of this introduction to discuss them. It is important, however, to acknowledge that they exist and over the last thirty years have promoted an ongoing and intense scholarly and political discussion. And that they remain unresolved.

Slang by its nature does not make, or does not set out to make, a political statement. In the case of the language of gay and lesbian people, this is not the case. In his review of such language in 2000, the scholar Don Kulick confessed himself at a loss, admitting that even the naming of these 'nonheteronormative' communities was problematic, but that given the importance of naming as a fundamental of existence, it had to be considered. The word *gay*, once used without argument, had been discarded; the term *queer*, recaptured from those who used it derogatively, was still too offensive for many. The acronym *LGBTTSQ*—Lesbian, Gay, Bisexual, Transgendered, Two-Spirit, Queer, or Questioning—seemed too cumbersome and might not cover the entirety of the non-heterosexual waterfront. In the end, he fell back on standard English: gay and lesbian.

For the historian of slang things are simpler. Initial references to the homosexual—around 310 terms for male homosexuals, 130 for lesbians—within my database are to an object: the object of others' disdain or fear (and perhaps lust, though well disguised). Typically in the 18th-century phrase 'bestial back-sliding', a synonym for homosexuality that combines physical distaste with pulpit admonition. First noted in the 16th century, this negative attitude and the linguistic practise it underpins lasts well into modernity. Not until the 20th century does one start to see the words used *by* homosexuals. A variety of glossaries are assembled, the first in 1910, and gay language starts to appear in fiction in the 1920s. The advent of activist Gay Liberation in the late 1960s changed the nature both of the language and of the way in which it was discussed. This intensified around 1980, since when, as noted, a wide-ranging discussion, mainly within the academic/ activist world, has dominated the subject.

In common again with 'heterosexual' or rather general slang, the gay lexis offers a set of long-running themes. Old and young men; parts of the body, notably the penis and its dimensions; sexual intercourse (in this case anal); man-to-man fellatio; sexual preferences (especially as appended to the all-purpose suffix *-queen*). The 'out-group', in general slang often a naive or gullible countryman, is represented by heterosexuals. The construction of many terms also shows the regular use of female names for men (but without the prejudicial sense that is part of the 'straight' use of such terms to describe gay men) and the 'feminization' of male sexual terms, often simply reversing the gender use of words that, for instance, might be used for the vagina and for man-to-woman cunnilingus and applying them to the penis and homosexual fellatio.

What is still acknowledged as the outstanding dictionary of gay slang appeared in 1972: *The Queen's Vernacular* by Bruce Rodgers. It remains, as Don Kulik put it, 'the magnificent, still unsurpassed Mother of all gay glossaries,... making all previous attempts to document gay slang look like shopping lists scribbled on the back of a paper bag'. It offers 12,000 entries, and Rodgers claimed to have conducted many interviews and taken many years to assemble his lists.

For the *Queen's Vernacular* Rodgers wrote a brief introduction. It sets the lexicon very much in its time: standing at the junction between the linguistic verbosity of the world of queens (for whom the book is of course named) and the new austerity of gay liberation, whose activists equated the use of traditional gay slang with volunteering to accept oppression. Rodgers looked back and forward. On the one hand he lauds the lexis he had collected, which, far from representing acquiescence, flaunts its own rebellion:

> [It] was invented, coined, dished and shrieked by the gay stereotypes. The flaming faggot, men who look like women, flagrant wrist-benders, the women who don't shave their legs, all those who find it difficult to be accepted for what they feel they are even within the pariah gay subculture. And they stereotype others because they themselves have been labeled offensively.... They jeer because they have been mocked; they retaliate with a barrage of their own words which ridicule women, male virility, the sanctity of marriage,

everything in life from which they are divorced. Such words 'enrich…our language immensely' as well as serving as the queen's form of protest.

Nonetheless he accepts that slang is a product of the ghetto and 'those who struggle to leave the ghetto shake off its language first'. He acknowledged that 'many gay militants are avidly opposed to this contrived lingo with which the oppressed faggot makes himself understood, and then only to a "sister." They consider the jargon yet another link in the chain which holds the homosexual enslaved.'

It is this dichotomy that has dominated the status of 'gay slang' since the 1970s and even more so since the 1980s. It has led to paper and counter-paper and glosses on both, and after that new papers to augment or replace those. The struggle, in various senses, continues.

Polari

If gay slang is a subset of a larger non-standard lexis, Polari is a subset of gay usage. Known originally as *lingua franca*, in the original Italian, 'the language of the Franks', i.e. French, it was born as a form of hybrid tongue, based on Occitan and Italian and used in the Mediterranean for trading and military purposes. 'Lingua Franca' currently refers to traders' pidgin, but in 17th-century Britain it began to gain an alternative role: a synonym for the language, properly a jargon or 'professional slang', used (among other vocabularies) by tramps, sailors, show people, and (somewhat later) homosexuals. In this role it gained a new name, variously spelt *parlyaree*, *palarie*, and, for the purposes of this discussion, *polari*. It was outrageous, in-your-face camp, and deliberately so.

The move from trade to *trade* seems to have come via the sea, thence the stage, and finally the gay world that linked to both. The pre-Gay Liberation male homosexual world, like any 'secret' subgroup of society, both required and desired some form of 'secret' language, working simultaneously to affirm the secret unity of the outcast and by 'speaking in tongues' to hide from the larger, hostile world. Polari, picked up from seafaring pals or adopted from the theatre, fitted the bill.

Polari has never really been a 'proper' language. It had no grammar or syntax and relied without difficulty on recognized English forms. Even at its 1950s peak it was at best a lexicon, barely more than a hundred terms in all. Although Polari refuses completely to die, it was severely bruised by the macho style of Gay Liberation. The limp wrist was declared taboo; using any form of camp language, however useful it might have been to a subculture which accepted, even if reluctantly, the oppression it faced, was simply affirming the justice of that oppression. It was another facet of the closet, and it had to go.

Chapter 6
The components of slang

Forms

Slang offers no forms unique to itself. Cheerfully borrowing much of its lexis from standard English it employs similar methods of constructing it. The simplest, and most popular use is in varieties of combining, whether as phrases, compounds, or derivatives. Of its 54,000 headwords, some 5,700 are employed as the basis of 19,300 phrases and 3,700 headwords provide the roots of 18,200 compounds. There are 1,100 nested derivatives, but the form can be found in many more stand-alone examples. Slang also offers a number of infixes, notably *-fucking-*, *-bloody-*, and the *-iz* use created in swing music and recently popular in rap. Prefixes focus on *ker-*, *ka-*, and *ca-*, usually denoting some form of sudden noise or movement.

Slang also makes use of clipping (*abfab, bourgie, combo*), initialism (*G&T, B&S, NSIT*), and acronyms (*bae, snafu,* and *c.r.e.a.m.*) There are blends (*bootylicious, grabtastic, fugly, wanksta*). The vocabulary includes both loanwords proper (*boocoos, parlay, mungaree, blouzabella,* plus a good many Yiddishisms) and loan translations (*bad-eye, badmouth, give me some skin*). Proper names may be eponymic, as most commonly seen in numbers of rhyming slang terms, as well as such 'characters' as *Jody* (i.e. the wife- or partner-stealing 'Joe de grinder'), *Aunt Mary* (menstruation), and *Mr Charlie*, and as plays on well-known brands such as *adidas* ('all day I dream about sex'), a *coke frame* (the curvaceous female form that supposedly resembles a Coca-Cola bottle), or *McJob* (a 'junk' job). Onomatopoeia is common, as in terms for vomiting: *huey* or *Ralph*. Finally, and particularly associated with rap, conferring a wholly self-conscious 'illiteracy' on its speakers, are respellings: *gangsta, balla, flava, sista,* etc.

Etymological roots

The etymology of the word 'slang' is complex. That of the slang lexis, with a few notable exceptions, far less so. On the whole the meaning is derived from what can be done to a word rather than pondering its linguistic root.

Slang, and cant before it, has always been promiscuous in its accretion of sources. At the time of writing my current database runs to approximately 54,000 headword entries (derivations, compounds, and phrasal uses bringing the total slang lexis to something around 130,000 terms). Setting aside some 33 per cent of the etymologies which cross-refer to another slang headword, the first and foremost of these sources is standard English, the twisting, tweaking, and otherwise ludic exploitation of which accounts for at least 15 per cent of the vocabulary. In terms of register rhyming slang and abbreviations offer around 5 per cent each, and lesser roles are played by puns and plays on words (*c.*1400 entries), dialect (870 entries), proper names (375 entries), echoic uses (257 entries), and brand-names (90 entries). In terms of languages, the most influential has been French with 400 etymologies, followed by Scottish (305), Latin (241), Irish (220), Afrikaans (212), Yiddish (199), German (195), Italian (162), Dutch (152), Romani (117), Hindi (79), Hebrew (44), Greek (40), Welsh (31), Twi (25), Spanish (21), Zulu (20), Yoruba (14), and Arabic (7). These are of course immediate etymologies, and the range and depth of languages might be substantially multiplied were the slang lexicographer to go up (or perhaps down) one level further and append the roots of the standard English words that lie behind so much slang. For the purposes of slang dictionaries, however, this is omitted.

And although slang is seen as 'trendy' or 'cutting edge', its call on events, on the immediacy of anecdotes, is relatively tiny. If there is anywhere that this, at least in an extended form which overlaps with slang's use of proper names, is common, then it is in rhyming slang, where a variety of celebrities gained an extra reward via the form. Thus *Posh and Becks* (the popstrel-turned-fashionista Victoria and her husband, footballer David Beckham) are used to mean 'sex', the feminist *Germaine Greer* to mean 'beer', and so on. The tradition is well established and one finds long-departed stars offered the same treatment, e.g. the music hall entertainer *Wilkie Bard* for 'playing card', the footballer *Nobby Stiles* for 'piles', i.e. haemorrhoids, or the film star *Errol Flynn* for 'gin'. Otherwise the list of anecdotal roots is limited. One finds Australia's *blind Freddie*, in life the blind beggar Frederick Solomons (d. 1933), known as 'Blind Freddie' and who frequented the Sydney streets in the early 20th century. Slang adopted him to denote an imaginary figure seen as representing the lowest denominator of incompetence; thus used in phrases such as *blind Freddie could see that* or *wouldn't fool blind Freddie*. The originally nautical use of *Fanny Adams* to mean tinned mutton refers callously to the brutal murder and dismemberment of 8-year-old Fanny Adams, at Alton, Hampshire, on 24 August 1867; the murderer, one Frederick Baker, was hanged at Winchester on Christmas Eve; 5,000 people watched his execution. *Jimmy Woods*, Australia's emblematic solo drinker, comes from a poem of 1892, but thereafter he is fictional. Other terms that seem to demand a story prove dead ends. We have *Billy Harran's dog*, *Joe Heath's mare*, and *Paddy Ward's pig*; *Dolan's ass* and *Tom Bray's bilk*, *drunk as Cooter Brown*, but if these were ever well-known people rather than mysterious generics, their fame has vanished.

Certain areas combine proper names and puns: they are not anecdotal as such and the lexicographer can only offer the simple definition: an example is *betty*, used for a small crowbar used to force doors. There appears no reason for this use of a proper name, a diminutive of Elizabeth, other than the tool's size. But the use of this particular female name seems arbitrary. It only assumes a logical sense when ranked as part of a group (*jenny*, *billy*, *jemmy*, *jimmy*) all of which refer to a prying tool. The most recent is the *slim jim*. The earliest version, *jenny*, suggests an abbreviation of the standard English *engine*, but this formation is not currently recorded until the 'spinning jenny' appears in 1789. Thereafter we are simply looking at quasi-punning nicknames, based on Elizabeth, William, or James. There is no innate 'pryingness' that can be traced to any of them. Another group of crowbars: the *citizen*, *gentleman*, *alderman*, and *lord mayor*, are nicknames too, and the hierarchy is consciously nodding to the ascending size of the tool.

Some terms—this is hardly limited to slang—continue to defy the etymologist. Perhaps 1,000 of the database's 130,000 are marked 'etymology unknown'. Some have produced a range of theories, notably such perennial sources of debate as *kibosh*, *the whole nine yards*, or *posh*, but they remain unproven. Slang also attracts a regular supply of popular, for which read erroneous if much-loved, etymologies, often based on confected acronyms, among them that for *fuck*: 'fornicate under command of the King'. More alluring, but still a non-starter, was the attribution of *hokey-pokey*, a cheap variety of ice-cream peddled by Italian vendors sometimes doubling as organ-grinders, to the Italian *o che poco!* 'o how little!'; more likely is a link to *hokey-pokey*, meaning swindling and a form of the far older *hocus-pocus*, in this case the passing off of a cheap simulacrum of a superior product.

If a guess can be made at some of the 'unknowns', some remain obdurate. Why, for instance does *grote* mean an informer? Why did *modock* once stand for one who became an aviator for the social prestige or publicity, what made a *weejee* into a chimney-pot, and why exactly does *zebbled*, at least at UK schools, mean uncircumcised?

Validity

The dependence on lexicography and thus lexicographers, plus an insufficiency of records and concomitant lack of accurate dating, leads to a further problem: how does one validate the terms presented?

Sometimes such terms seem consciously artificial. The London printer John Duncombe, whose presses turned out a good deal of mid-19th-century pornography, issued a slang dictionary around 1850. It has such entries as *caddock*, the stomach, to *elk*, to give a loan, *ravellavern*, a person who steals luggage from travelling coaches, and *swapperchop-brammums*, a bank. There is a group that use the preface *abb-*, all referring to prison: *abb-clouts*—prison dress, *abb-discipline*—whipping in the prison courtyard, either publicly or without witness, *abb-gammonry*—a condemned sermon, *abb-tanger*—the passing bell at execution, and *abb-whack*—jail allowance. Why *abb* (which turns up as *ab*s in another set) should mean prison (the nearest equivalent is the Latin *ab*: from, by, since, and of) does not, as they say, compute. The sole possibility is *abbot*, meaning prison warden, but this appears only in Duncombe, and in Kent's canting dictionary that he published in 1835, and Kent makes no reference to *abbs* in any form. Duncombe also includes what he terms 'the Cracksman's new mode of counting'; it runs 1 *Yunibec* 2 *Twibecs* 3 *Tribecs* 4 *Katrambecs* 5 *Knimtrambecs* 6 *Hexambecs* 7 *Septzambecs* 8 *Octzambecs* 9 *Nouxambecs* 10 *Dyams*, and goes on to 500. None of these terms have survived, other than in subsequent dictionaries. We can still admire Duncombe's inventiveness. Isn't this, in its way, an example of perfect slang: absolutely incomprehensible other than to its users? Unfortunately, as regards hard evidence of their use, there is none to be found.

At the same time a term listed in a given dictionary may offer neither provenance nor subsequent examples. It may not be a nonce-word (a one-off use), but there is no tangible proof. Of the 1,100-odd entries for which the seven-volume Victorian slang dictionary Farmer & Henley's *Slang and its Analogues* provides a first use, around 75 per cent have yet to be recorded again. The authors offer citations for some of these entries, but far from all (typically in their magisterial lists of synonyms for intercourse) and there is no Bibliography available. It is hard for a successor to assess such terms usefully.

The problem is not, however, restricted to the past. If anything it has intensified on-line. Today, with too much, rather than too little information, we still face the same question. The traditional dictionary, using citations and latterly corpora for its evidence, can hope to back up its headwords with tangible proof, ideally with multiple uses of a given word or phrase. A digital database, such as that of the *Urban Dictionary*, which as of January 2014 boasted 7 million definitions (garnered over a fifteen-year lifetime), and accepts a further 2,000 uploads each day, dwarfs even the *OED*, and shames even the most comprehensive slang dictionary in print. The question for the traditionalist, or even the user who demands some degree of proof, is to what extent this tsunami of neologisms can be trusted. If Duncombe, in 1850, seemed to be making it up as he went along, plucking his entries from thin air, are the terms that appear in the *Urban Dictionary* any more dependable, given that many such uploads have no backing beyond the individual who submits them?

Multiple imagery

In parallel to variant spellings are variant, if closely connected, images. Slang comes up with a single image which having been accepted as suitable for a given definition launches others. The users see no reason to maintain a canonical form, and as ever, play with what is available. The underlying term *horizontal refreshment*, found in 1843 as meaning sexual intercourse, has developed into *horizontal barn-dancing, . . . bop, . . . dancing, . . . exercise, . . . folk-dancing, . . . handshake, . . . jogging, . . . mambo, . . . polka, . . . polo, . . . relaxation, . . . rhumba, . . . rumble, . . . tango, . . . twist and shout*, and *. . . two-step*. The *horizontal worker* is thus a prostitute, and to *get horizontal* to have sex. However *horizontal pleasure*, used among World War II US troops who had more immediate priorities, means only sleep.

Agglomerations such as these, and slang offers many, are smaller-scale examples of slang's wider synonymies, and it seems that once a pattern is accepted, all suggested combinations are justifiable.

Euphemism

Such collections can also spring from a perceived need for euphemism (Figure 9). Given its preoccupation with sex and defecation, many of the long lists of synonyms that have gathered around these topics may be ascribed to a desire to indicate the general rather than the specific, and there is an abundance of what the Monty Python team would have termed 'nudge-nudge, wink-wink' about many such lists. However in certain cases the euphemism derives not from a theme, but from the need to avoid spelling out a certain taboo term.

The obscene term *motherfucker*, 'the ocdipal polysyllable', is generally ranked as among the 'dirtiest' of its type. First recorded in 1918 it had probably been in use since the 1890s. The supreme term of personal abuse, which is equally aimed at inanimate objects, it also works neutrally with a wide variety of meanings, from good to bad, often as a black-to-black term of affection or a compliment. It can mean an object or place, with no judgement implied; it may be used as an indefinite standard of comparison, or to denote a large or outstanding example. With so much 'work' available, but underpinned by its obscene origins, aside from a

THE GREAT SOCIAL EVIL.

Time:—Midnight. A Sketch not a Hundred Miles from the Haymarket.

Bella. "Ah! Fanny! How long have you been *Gay*?"

9. 'How Long Have You Been Gay?' Two less than cheery prostitutes underline slang's ironies in this mid-19th-century cartoon. Like so much slang, 'gay' ran through a variety of meanings before arriving at its current definition.

number of variant spellings—*mahthafukker, m'fucka, mothafucka, motherfugger, muh-fugger, muthafucka*—it has generated a vast range of at least ostensibly euphemistic substitutes:

> double-clutcher, emeff, futhermucker, granny-jazzer, mafa,
> mama-huncher, mama-jabber, mama-jammer, mammy-dogger,
> mammy-dugger, mammy-jammer, mammy-jammy, mammy-rammer,
> mammy-tapper, mary frances, maw-dicker, melon-farmer,
> mickey-fickey, Mister Franklin, mo dicker, mofo, molly wopper,
> molly-dodger, momma-hopper, momma-hopper, mother-bugger,
> mother-feryer, mother-flicker, mother-flunker, mother-for-you,
> mother-fouler, mother-fuyer, mother-grabber, mother-hopper,
> mother hubbard, mother-hubber, mother-hugger, mother-humper,
> mother-huncher, mother-jiver, mother-jumper, mother-lover,
> mother-plugger, mother-raper, mother-rubber, mother-sucker,
> mother superior, motheren, motherfrigger, motherhead, motheroo,
> motorcycle, muddy funster, mugger-bugger, mugger-fugger, and
> triple-clutcher.

Repetition tends to defuse impact, but it is surely hard not to acknowledge the power of these underlying dozen letters, so necessary has it been both to use them, but to sidestep, to however nominal an extent, their potent actuality.

Homonyms and other multiples

The variations on a single word—spelt the same, looks the same, but listed separately—are known as homonyms: words that sound and spell alike but have different meanings; this is not the same as the different senses that can be found within the same word. Slang provides many examples: there are, for instance, twenty-one separate *jack* nouns plus *the jack* and six verbs. Drawing lines between them is based on their deeper meaning whether in SE or in slang. Thus *jack* n.[5], a sailor, comes from *jack tar*, but *jack* n.[12], the anus, comes from *jacksie*. Senses are grouped at a single homonym, thus *jack* n.⁴, has three senses: a farthing, a generic for money in general, and in the Australian game of two-up, in which one bets on how a pair of tossed coins fall, a double-headed coin.

Certain terms reveal themselves to be epitomes of multi-tasking. Cant provided a matched pair of adjectives: *rum*, meaning good (at least in criminal terms) and *queer* meaning bad (on the same basis). There were 138 compounds and phrases based on rum and 133 based on queer. Between them they provided a comprehensive guide to the ups and downs of the villain's world. Still extant and equally productive is *hot*, an epitome of slang's subversion of a standard English term, which has 134 varieties on offer.

Etymologists dealing in standard English look to what are called linguistic *cognates*, defined by the *OED* as 'descended from the same original language; of the same linguistic family. Of words: Coming naturally from the same root, or representing the same original word, with differences due to subsequent separate phonetic development.' Slang looks at cognates too, but of a different variety: the relationship is not so much semantic but thematic. It is about the links between repeating imagery rather than the search for common linguistic roots. The ways in which the essential playing with different standard English words is linked not by the words themselves, but to their original meaning. For instance the various stereotypes of 'dog' that lie behind the uses of the basic word. Or a group of terms that both mean sexual intercourse and simultaneously suggest the world of do-it-yourself: *grind, screw, nail, plank, hammer, drill, bore, scrape, rasp, shaft*, and, simplest of all, *bang*.

Given slang's equation of many terms for intercourse with violence, 'man hits woman', this is logical enough. Not everything is so simple. Take the term *sharge*. We are not helped by the sole example of this, in a dictionary, but it is a defined as 'to copulate'. Why? because, it appears, that *sharge* is also dialect and the dialect meant to grind and to *grind*…

All words, or all words that fail to identify themselves at once, are subjected to this thematic filter. Terms that mean 'mad' or 'eccentric' will often suggest that the subject is 'not all there', terms that deal with drunkenness imply physical instability. Many are self-evident, others can be subject to reverse engineering. The endurance of this multiple synonymity and its fundamental role within slang offers rival interpretations: on the one hand one can see it as a means of avoiding the real world (as represented by SE) by conjuring up an infinity of parallel terms. On the other it suggests a better means, by offering up so many possible descriptions, of burrowing deeper inside it.

Chapter 7
Recording slang

Defining slang terms

What does a slang term mean? The answer is often obvious, but not invariably. The same word can stand in for multiple meanings, some barely differentiated from others. The task of discerning these differences, of dividing them into senses, is not helped, of course, by the core nature of the language under analysis. Slang is innately imprecise. Its use suggests fluidity and malleability. Its speakers are not grasping at linguistic precision. Not so much a matter of that obscurantism, that in-group secrecy that allegedly underpins much of slang's vocabulary, but more a matter of a lack of interest. The speaker is not thinking in terms of records, of the dictionary-maker's use of citations to elicit and establish meaning. For the latter context becomes all-important. Not just a matter of what does a given word mean, but how is it meant *here*? The dependence of so much slang on tweaked standard English is of no help. A *pipe* may on occasion actually be just that: a pipe. But let us assume that it is definitely not, though, as we shall see, even that assumption is something of a false friend.

The first task is to group the various senses. There are those that deal with the reproduction of sound via the physical shape of the throat, a pipe, amplified by windpipe. It can be the human voice, the song that it sings, and a story that is told. It can be a telephone or a saxophone. The next group tweak the SE again, looking to the pipe as a tube, but this time depend mainly on double entendre for sexual reference: the penis and the vagina; although the shape, devoid of sniggering, also gives top-boots. Next come drug uses, where the pipe is, indeed, a pipe. A cigar, an opium pipe, and which, as pipe or the pipe, represent the smoking of opium and as pipe again an opium smoker, a marijuana or hashish pipe, and a smoker of either; a vein into which a drug can be injected (which reflects the 17th-century *pipe-vein*, a human vein) and finally a pipe for smoking base cocaine or crack and, by metonymy, the drug itself. A fourth group uses the slang phrase, a lead-pipe cinch, to give the meaning of a certainty or something that is easily accomplished; a fifth, based on the specific lead pipe, gives any form of clubbing weapon and finally, in London and constructed with *the*, the River Thames.

Obviously some of these are not going to be confused; the saxophone and the Thames, the penis and the certainty make their identity clear. But the variations on drug uses, the fine-tuning of the meanings pertaining to sound, these require the sanctification of context and thus citation.

Spelling slang

Spelling and pronunciation are not really considered by slang's speakers. Writers and lexicographers, however, need some form of transcribing what they hear. Given slang's dependence on standard English, the accuracy of spelling can be assumed in many cases, but far from all. The more a word or phrase appears to have been deliberately invented, a category that tends to focus on the underworld, where conscious neologism is or certainly was the norm, the more likely it is to defy any unarguable orthography.

Of the near-54,000 headwords I have gathered, almost 11,000 offer alternative forms. In many cases these are not so much alternative spellings but represent a variation on the primary form, i.e. *hookem-snivey*, which can mean a trick or to deceive, is also recorded as *hook-and-snivey*, *hook-and-snivvy*, *hook 'em snivey*, and *hokum-snivey*. It is an odd phrase; its variations are hardly surprising. Its use must have been almost entirely in speech; there are only seven contemporary examples, irrespective of spelling, set down in print and all these are glossarial. (Beyond cant it was adopted as a proper name, 'Hookem Snivey the famous fortune-teller', as well as that of a country village and a boat, but these are coincidental.) *Marihoochie*, a jocular take on *marijuana*, appears variously as *marahoochie*, *marihooch*, *marihootee*, *marihootie*, and *marijooani*. The alternatives merely play further with the primary term and all, perhaps, mock the 'straight' user's problem with pronunciation.

The question remains: the word is heard, how is it to be set down? Take, for instance, *monniker*, which since the mid-19th century has meant 'a name', and emerged from criminal usage. It remains in use, if somewhat anachronistically. Its etymology is unproven, with some seeing it as a development of *monogram* and others, such as Eric Partridge, suggesting a link to *monarch*, a king or queen, who like a given name 'rules' the individual life. The *OED*, which claims the earliest version to be the 18th century's *monarch* but offers no examples, adds the suggestion of a possible backslang version of *eke-name*, literally an 'additional name' and itself the root of *nickname*. Its spellings, derived from a variety of cited uses, include *monacher*, *monack*, *monacker*, *monacre*, *monaker*, *monarch*, *monekeer*, *moneker*, *monekur*, *monica*, *monicher*, *monick*, *monicker*, *monika*, *moniker*, *monikey*, *monker*, *monnick*, *monoger*, and *nomaker*. This may not be a complete list. Henry Mayhew, using the term in his *Morning Post* series on London poverty, published between 1841 and 1851, opted for *monekur*. So too did his brother Augustus, using it in a novel in 1858. Meanwhile Henry had changed his mind, preferring *monekeer* in 1856. Examples taken from dictionaries, newspapers, fiction, and reportage fill out the list. Recent use seems to have settled on *moniker* or *monicker*.

To what extent slang's spelling actually matters is arguable. Henry Mayhew, after all, seemed unperturbed by his own inconsistency and he is hardly alone. Writers of fiction or journalism may well feel the same; meanwhile the lexicographer, with the task of accurate recording, remains keen, here as elsewhere, to offer 'truth'.

On occasion, however rarely, slang's spelling has more to offer and can both clarify and confuse the issue. The classic example being slang's version of the buttocks: *arse* in English slang, *ass* in American.

The earliest use of *arse*, albeit as *ers*, is found in 1000 where in a Latin-to-Anglo-Saxon glossary it translates the Latin *podex*; it is in general use from around 1300 and gradually moves from standard, in common with various other 'obscenities', into slang. Shakespeare has it in *Romeo and Juliet* (1595), 'Oh Romeo! that she were, oh, that she were an open arse, thou a poperin pear,' though this combines various puns (*open-arse*, a medlar, supposedly from the resemblance of the fruit and buttocks; *poperin* from Poperinghe, in west Flanders and 'pop her in'). The American spelling, first recorded in a joke-book of 1761, seems to emerge as a pun: 'An old woman had a jack ass run away...she called out to a man in the road, stop my ass master, stop me ass. Take a cork you old whore, and stop it yourself, say he.' But Shakespeare also uses the *ass* spelling as useful in puns. And while early uses of ass meaning a fool, based on a stereotyped donkey, are generally clear, modern examples, at least from America, are less easy to discern. The Americanization of modern UK slang compounds the issue: supposedly 'English' examples having been coming with an American spelling since the 1990s.

Dating slang

Dating of all words is mutable. The lexicographer can only offer what is known. The continual increase of material made available on-line is revolutionizing the situation, but no single lexicographer, nor even a many-handed team, can ever hope to read and dissect it all, and 'all' increases daily. Until everything useful has been scanned, digitized, and made available for search, the essential serendipity that has always lain behind even the most hopefully comprehensive of reading lists will play its role.

For slang this is compounded by the innate marginality of the lexis placed beneath the microscope. The composition of a lexis starts with the words that make it up, what a dictionary would term its headwords. The early history of the lexis is too often limited to its early lexicography: the beggar books, a selection of more or less voyeuristic pamphlets, and, in fiction, a number of plays and 'true confessions'. Unlike that of standard English slang's 'childhood' lacks good records. The original *OED*, for all its comprehensive reading lists and battalions of voluntary readers, was still forced to depend over-heavily on earlier dictionaries for its slang examples. This has naturally changed, but as for any recorder of slang, those dictionaries still bulk large.

Like the dictionary, which is never finished, only paused for a publisher's deadline or the delivery of a new update to a website, dating is open-ended. Its accuracy is flexible, and the statement 'first use' is better stated as 'first currently recorded'.

Pronouncing slang

Slang dictionaries do not essay pronunciation guides. Phonology, originally defined as the science of pronunciation, is of course subjected to a wide range of studies, reaching back to the supposed sound of Shakespeare and beyond, but these are generally academic. If they help us with the pronunciation of slang, lexicographers, rightly or not, have yet to incorporate their findings.

It may be, as in the alternative transcriptions of *moniker*, that they suggest a variety of pronunciations, at least heard by the writer who set them down, but there is no guarantee. We know that the substitution of 'v' for 'w' and vice versa was not merely a Dickensian invention for his character Sam Weller but an everyday aspect of contemporary Victorian speech around the mid-19th century, but if we wish for an idea of the sounds of 16th-century cant or 18th-century flash we must extrapolate from wider data. Looking at the confected 'conversations' found in such as Harman, Moll King, or a selection of 19th-century introductions to London low-life, there is no attempt to transliterate. Mayhew's interviewees are sometimes offered Cockney speech patterns, but come with aspirates and final 'g's intact. The terminology alone provides slang or cant's specialism.

The v/w convention was a temporary one, and seems to have died out by the 1870s. Its appearance does, however, indicate that writers were concerned, perhaps for the first time, with offering an accurate transcription of lower-class speech. In his study *Cockney Past and Present* (1938) William Mathews notes that this had been an occasional preoccupation for several centuries, but it does not seem to have intensified until the 19th century.

The representations of Cockney speech naturally included slang on a variety of levels, and as well as quantity there was also the quality to be considered. There were a number of debates over how the sound of that slang, and of Cockney pronunciation in general, should appear on the page. Dickens, in the v/w substitutions of Tony and Sam Weller, did it one way, Milliken's cocky social climber 'Arry promoted another for *Punch* although his speech is mainly delineated by dropped aitches and such pronunciations as 'pooty' for *pretty* and 'perlite' for *polite*, and Ortheris, the Cockney member of Kipling's *Soldiers Three*, another. The Cockney novelists, aiming for accuracy whether they were portraying the violent or more sentimental image of the East End, refined things once more. The music hall had its own ways and it is possible to hear one of its stars, Gus Elen (albeit recorded thirty years after his prime), whose heavily accentuated pronunciation would typically render *lost* as 'lorst', *town* as 'tahn', *more* as 'mowah', and the phrase 'a great big shame' as something akin to 'a grite big shime'.

This succession of variations on distorted standard English was finally put to rest. Under the influence of the philologist Andrew Tuer, author of *The Kawkneigh Awlminek* (1883) and *Thenks awf'lly* (1890), there developed a full-scale phonetic system for transliteration, which has stayed in place ever since. Cockney itself remains in flux. Tuer's work sufficed for the white East Ender; now there is Estuary English, 'Mockney', and the multicultural tones of those whose roots lie very far from Petticoat Lane or the Isle of Dogs.

One aspect of representation remained impossible to overcome: the level of obscenity in Cockney speech. It was frustrating, and the writers often referred in their texts to their own need to self-bowdlerize, but they invariably held back. Arthur Morrison in *Tales of Mean Streets* (1894) came as near as was possible, using *bleedin'* and *bleeder*, and including such coarse abuse as calling women *cows* and *'eifers*, but the full-on obscenities remained far off limits. Even *bloody*, already acknowledged as the 'great Australian adjective' (though unprinted even in the poem of that name), is never used (other than by the pornographer 'Walter'). Dickens might use *blank* as did papers such as the *Sporting Times*, which expanded it to *blankety-blank*, but that was generally an American habit. Kipling used dashes.

Chapter 8
The lexicography of slang: slang's dictionaries

The standard dictionary, the dominant production of lexicography, deals with standard forms of language. Hard on their heels have come those of slang, collected for nearly half a millennium. It is impossible to list them all: the doyenne of slang collectors, Madeline Kripke of New York City, has amassed a library that currently numbers some 15,000 slang-related texts. There are, nonetheless, certain major examples, a slang lexicographical 'canon' as it were. It is these that will be considered here. This is, by necessity, a limited overview. For detailed study, readers are recommended to consult the four volumes (to date) of Prof. Julie Coleman's *History of Cant and Slang Dictionaries* (2004–), the outstanding authority.

England

Traditional English-language slang lexicography can be broken down into three successive periods. The 'canting' or criminal slang dictionaries of the 16th to 18th centuries, the 'vulgar tongue' works of the late 18th to mid-19th, and the 'modern' productions that have appeared since. One can now add a fourth: the collection and presentation of slang on-line.

The collection of 'cant' echoes the near-contemporary 'beggar-books' of Europe: designed to alert the law-abiding public to the existence of such beggars—'the canting crew'—listing their occupational types, and offering a small glossary of their language. The first such work was Robert Copland's *Hye Way to the Spytell House* (*c.*1535). In the form of a verse dialogue between the printer Copland and the porter of the Spytell House (a charity hospital) Copland notes and the Porter describes the various categories of beggars and thieves, as well as their tricks and frauds. There is no glossary as such, but some thirty-six terms are defined in the text. In 1561 John Awdeley, another printer, published *The Fraternitie of Vagabondes*. The brief (nine-page) work, offering forty-eight headwords, falls into three parts: the first deals with rural villains, the second with their urban cousins, and the third is Awdeley's list of 'the xxv. Orders of Knaues, otherwyse called a Quartern of Knaues'.

The most influential 16th-century work appears *c.*1566: Thomas Harman's *Caveat for Common Cursetors*. Harman, a magistrate, produced a consciously didactic work, designed to introduce the reader to 'the leud lousey language of these lewtering [loitering] luskes [idlers] and lasy lorrels [blackguards] where with they bye and sell the common people as they pas through the country. Whych language they terme Peddelars Frenche...' There are twenty-four small essays, each dealing with a different rank of villain, plus a list of some 114 terms. These are very briefly defined, usually with a single synonym. The *Caveat* concludes with a list of contemporary beggars and a specimen cant dialogue.

Harman's vocabulary would remain the core of several subsequent glossaries, with a succession of 'rogue pamphlets' appearing over the two centuries. Among these are *The Bellman of London* and *Lanthorne and Candlelight* (1608) by the playwright Thomas Dekker, and *Martin Mark-All, beadle of Bridewell* by Samuel Rowlands (or Rid), in 1610. Others include Richard Head's *The Canting Academy, or the Devil's Cabinet opened* (1673) and John Shirley's *Triumph of Wit* (1688).

While Harman can be seen as a sociological researcher, and Dekker et al. as informative reformers, the 'coney-catching' (i.e. confidence trickery) pamphlets of playwright Robert Greene are nakedly sensational. The first such pamphlet, *A Notable Discouery of Coosnage* [cozenage, or trickery]. *Now daily practised by sundry lewd persons called Connie-Catchers* [confidence tricksters] *and Cross-biters* [swindlers]…, appeared in 1591. Five sequels followed by 1592. Greene gleefully peddles his down-market sensationalism, larded with new canting terms—the vocabularies of the various branches of confidence trickery—and supposedly first-hand anecdote, but carefully quarantined with pious horror. In one pamphlet, *The Defence of Connycatching* 'by Cuthbert Conny-catcher', he even attacks himself.

With *A New Dictionary of the Terms ancient and modern of the Canting Crew*, by the anonymous B.E., Gent.[leman] (*c*.1698), there emerges the first major development in slang lexicography since Harman. B.E. remains an unknown figure, but his influence was substantial. It is the first ever stand-alone 'slang dictionary', rather than an appended glossary. The title emphasizes canting but B.E.'s vocabulary, some 4,000 words, adds general slang, colloquialisms, and a variety of non-criminal jargons to the core material.

There are terms from hunting, fencing, and duelling, and references to human intelligence, emotions, and physiognomy; to sports, games, jokes, and various forms of entertainment; to sex, to animals, to national and international politics, to religion, to warfare, and to seafaring, including smuggling and the language of shipbuilding. For some entries, however few, he offers citations and etymologies; there are a number of cross-references and he adopts usage labels.

Like Harman, B.E. would be 'honoured' by his plagiarists. These include Capt. Alexander Smith, whose *Thieves' New Canting*

Dictionary, included in his history of highwaymen (1719), is unashamedly derivative. Similarly the *New Canting Dictionary* (1725) is no more than an adaptation. The glossary attached to the oft-reprinted *Life* of the self-styled 'king of the gypsies' Bamfylde Moore Carew (1750 et seq.) is similarly sourced. Carew's tale made for a remarkably successful book. Its appeal is best summed up in the title of the expanded reissue, in 1749: *An Apology for the Life of Bamfylde-Moore Carew (Son to the Rev. Mr Carew of Bickley) commonly known throughout the West of England by the Title of King of the Beggars; and Dog-merchant-general. Containing an Account of his leaving Tiverton School at the Age of 15, and entering into a Society of Gypsies; his many and comical Adventures, more particularly a full and faithful Relation of his Travels twice thro' a great Part of America, his manner of living with the wild Indians, his bold Attempt in swimming the River Delaware, and many other extraordinary Incidents; his Return home, and Travels since, in England, Wales, Scotland and Ireland. The whole taken from his own mouth.* Sales were good enough for another, even longer, edition in 1750—the first to carry the canting glossary—and new editions, expanded by yet more picaresque adventures, appeared until 1779. The book was reprinted regularly throughout the 19th century, the last version appearing in 1882.

It was not until 1665 that the beggar book regained a major publication, with Richard Head's *The English Rogue*. This, the life-story of one Meriton Latroon (from *latron*: a robber), 'a witty extravagant', embellished with 'a Compleat History of the Most Eminent Cheats of Both Sexes', included a seven-page glossary, drawing freely on Harman and Dekker, and the canting song, 'Bing Out Bien Morts', which is dense with cant. Compared to beggar books, with their focus on taxonomy-plus-glossary, *The English Rogue*, with its many titillating or amusing episodes, is more in the jest-book tradition, or, given its focus on criminality, the more anecdotally based work of Greene, Dekker, and Rowlands. However Head is at pains to include and explicate cant: like those predecessors, he must have known how potent the thieves' vocabulary was in selling a book.

Eight years after the original Rogue came Head's solo offering: *The Canting Academy, or the Devil's Cabinet opened. Wherein is shown the mysterious and villainous practices of that wicked crew commonly known by the name of Hectors, Trepanners, Gilts, etc . . .* (1673). One extra aspect of the book is that, like a traditional bilingual dictionary, Head offers 'Standard English–Cant/Cant–Standard English' sections. Cant is presented not merely as a parallel vocabulary, but as a genuinely 'foreign' one.

More important was Head's wider influence. Mainstream lexicographers had so far averted their gaze from cant and similar vulgarisms. But three years after *The Canting Academy* appeared that pattern changed, albeit briefly. Elisha Coles published his *English Dictionary* in 1676. In it was included pretty much all of Head's word-list. Coles, unsurprisingly, felt it necessary to note in his preface his deviation from the orthodox. His justification is pleasingly pragmatic: "Tis no Disparagement to understand the Canting Terms: It may chance to save your Throat from being cut, or (at least) your Pocket from being pick'd.' The need to justify what might otherwise have been seen as titillatory commercialism was a constant.

Coles's innovation did not last. Samuel Johnson, eschewing anything that he considered naked vulgarity, had no truck with such material. Nathaniel Bailey, Johnson's immediate predecessor and sometime rival, did include some of the vocabulary, and offered a separate thirty-six-page list (drawn from B.E. via the *New Canting Dictionary*) in later editions of his *Universal Etymological English Dictionary*, but he was still the exception. A rare exception, and on the surface a surprising one, was *The Ladies Dictionary*, written by the well-known London bookseller John Dunton and published in 1694. This work, which aimed at being 'a Compleat Directory to the Female-Sex in all Relations,

Companies, Conditions and States of Life', did include some cant vocabulary, essentially that referring to the ranks of female beggars. Its aim, presumably, was to acquaint its gentle readers with the varieties of female mendicants they might find at their doors.

The 18th century did not merely produce adaptations of B.E. The voyeuristic popularity of the underworld, proven in embryo by the beggar books and 'coney-catching' pamphlets that followed them, continued. Paradoxically the era's most full-on peep into crime, John Gay's *The Beggar's Opera* (1728), almost avoided all slang. This was in direct contrast to its predecessor, Thomas Shadwell's *Squire of Alsatia* (1688), which had offered a glossary to aid the audience's understanding of the cant-heavy script.

Among other works, all offering glossaries, are *Hell Upon Earth* (1703), *The Memoirs of the right villainous John Hall* (1708), *The Amorous Gallant's Tongue*, by 'G.L.' (1710 et seq.), *The Regulator* (1718) by Claude Hitchens, Daniel Defoe's *Street Robberies Considered* (1728), James Dalton's *Genuine Narrative of Street Robberies Considered* (1728), the confessional *Discoveries of John Poulter* (1753), and George Parker's *View of Society in High and Low Life* (1781) and *Life's Painter of Variegated Characters* (1789).

The work of George Parker (1732–1800), self-appointed 'Librarian to the College of Wit, Mirth and Humour', was published in the 1780s, long after the genre had seemingly disappeared, but its content makes it the last of the beggar books. The *View of Society* offers an analysis of the world and language, of a wide range of professional thieves. Like his 17th-century predecessors, Parker positioned himself as a reporter. Joining a group of beggars in Dunkirk, he travels with them and notes no less than seventy-four discrete varieties of villain, plus their special techniques. Like Greene and Dekker long before, he gives a detailed run-down of their activities, although there is no glossary as such.

Life's Painter (1789) proclaimed its aim of exposing 'these invaders of our property, our safety, and our lives, who have a language quite unintelligible to any but themselves, and an established code of laws productive of their common safety at the same time, and live in splendour without the exertion of industry, labour, or care'. In its fifteenth chapter Parker lays out a list of some 125 terms, along with illustrative anecdotes. Among the 'variegated characters' is one group particularly worthy of note: '*Slang Boys. Boys of the slang*: fellows who speak the *slang language*, which is the same as *flash* and *cant*.' Flash and slang were not exactly the same as cant: the former had replaced it and the latter expanded into a far larger social arena, but Parker could see what was to come.

In 1785 arrives the next way-station in slang collection: *The Classical Dictionary of the Vulgar Tongue*, by the antiquary and former militia officer Captain Francis Grose. A second, substantially augmented edition appeared in 1788, followed by a third in 1796, the pirated Lexicon *Balatronicum* (effectively the fourth) in 1811, and the fifth, edited by the boxing journalist Pierce Egan, in 1823. In his 4,000 headwords Grose incorporates his main predecessors, but expands much further into general slang, his 'vulgar tongue'.

Grose's work made it even more clear that there was more to slang than the professional jargon of thieves and beggars. Cant's usual suspects are duly rounded up—*abram-cove, autem bawler, bawdy basket, bene darkmans*, and their roguish like—all culled from the 16th-century glossaries, but like B.E. he has taken on board the larger world of general slang. In Grose the reader has moved beyond the surreptitious whispering of 16th- and 17th-century villainy and into the wider arena, where 'civilians', as well as crooks, use the 'parallel' vocabulary of slang.

What Grose had done was to remove slang from its association with criminals and put it, with a much enlarged lexis, into the mouths of the common people. On occasion he did this literally, taking terms that had been labelled as cant and redefining them as 'vulgar'. Like B.E. he finds a place for a good deal of what would now be defined as occupational jargon, whether the words of soldiers and sailors or those of Billingsgate fishwives, long celebrated for the acerbity, not to mention coarseness of their epithets. For Grose this vulgar tongue was an essential part of British freedom: in this case of speech. Not for Britain the artificial restraints of the Académie Française and similar 'un-British' institutions. Garrick had praised Johnson for his success when with his *Dictionary* he had 'beat forty French and could beat forty more' (the number being that of the members of the Académie). Grose's dictionary, while unsung, attained a similar image of Britishness.

The third edition of Grose's dictionary, published in 1796, provides an unrivalled checklist of the level of slang's expansion as the 18th century draws to a close. Slang has by now spread hugely from its original emergence. Setting aside the 400-odd canting terms, still working from the 16th-century core, the major themes that inform slang are all well established. The world of alcohol offers 165 terms, that of the genitals and buttocks 325, and sexual intercourse a further 200; 130 terms stand for fools and the foolish, there are 220 prostitutes working in 40 brothels and accompanied by 35 pimps. Men and women of assorted types are good for 160 terms apiece. Terms for the mad, the fat, and the unattractive are still relatively limited; none exceeds 20 synonyms, but there are 42 oaths and 30 thugs.

Grose now set the pattern for the next century. As well as Pierce Egan's 1823 revision of Grose, that year also saw a lexicon 'of the Turf, the Ring, the Chase, the Pit, of Bon Ton and the Varieties of Life'. Its author was 'Jon Bee' (properly John Badcock), who had already challenged Egan's best-selling chronicle of *Life in London* (1821) with his own hugely derivative *Real Life in London* (1821). Badcock's book is far more verbose than Egan's, but lexicographically it is more curiosity than linguistic tool.

Four more noteworthy dictionaries appear by 1900. The first, in 1857, is the brief *Vulgar Tongue* by 'Ducange Anglicus'. It comprises a pair of glossaries, the first collected by the author, the second from a report presented to the government in 1839. It is the first to offer rhyming slang. In 1859 appeared the first of the six editions (variously expanded) of John Camden Hotten's *Modern Slang, Cant and Vulgar Words*, latterly *The Slang Dictionary*. Hotten was variously a bookseller/publisher, a pirate of such American 'stars' as Mark Twain, and a cultivator of his 'flower garden', books of flagellant pornography. His *Dictionary* has lists of rhyming slang and of backslang, both prefaced by a brief history and discussion. There is, for the first time, a 'Bibliography of Slang and Cant', with his own critical comments on each. Hotten stresses that this is above all a dictionary of 'modern Slang—a list of colloquial words and phrases in present use—whether of ancient or modern formation'. He omits obsolete terms and has opted to exclude 'filthy and obscene words' although he acknowledges their prevalence in street-talk. He touches on jargon and deals with the terminology of the beau monde, politics, the army and navy, the Church, the law, literature, and the theatre. He has a list of slang terms for money, one of oaths, one for drunkenness, and deals with the language of shopkeepers and workmen.

Hotten was *the* slang dictionary until 1890. His pre-eminence was somewhat breached in 1889 by *The Dictionary of Slang, Jargon and Cant* by Albert Barrère and C. G. Leland. But this two-volume work was barely published when it was displaced, by the seven volumes of John Farmer and W. E. Henley's *Slang and its Analogues* (1890–1904, rev. edn. vol. 1, 1909). Farmer, who combined slang researches with writings on spiritualism, and Henley, then one the Britain's leading poets, took slang lexicography into a new dimension. The book adopted the same 'historical' method as the contemporaneous *New English Dictionary*. All but a few headwords come with a number of citations, some 100,000 in all, set out as in a standard English dictionary, to illustrate usage and nuance. There are substantial lists of synonyms: those listed at *monosyllable* (the vagina), for instance, run to thirteen columns, while those at *greens* (sexual intercourse) run to seven. There are errors, typically in the citations, where dates and even the quotes themselves may have fallen foul of the sheer volume of the undertaking, but the overall achievement of Farmer and Henley far outweighs such slips.

To list the collections of 20th- and 21st-century slang is impossible. The range, from massively researched multi-volumed 'historical' dictionaries, to fly-by-night glossaries posted on the Internet, defies cataloguing. Nor is it possible to restrict 'English' slang to England. While Eric Partridge could entitle his book, based originally on Farmer and Henley, whose rights were owned by his publisher, as the *Dictionary of Slang and Unconventional English* (1937 et seq.) and exclude terms from America, such exclusivity would now be foolhardy. Similarly Australian slang, pioneered by the mid-20th-century work of Sidney J. Baker, has an important presence. The mass media, the Internet, the role of English, or certainly Englishes, as a world language mean that its slang is equally multi-headed and its dictionaries reflect the fact.

Partridge dominated much of the 20th century. His is perhaps a flawed canon, his lexicographical method was less than wholly scrupulous, his inability to keep personal comment out of his definitions less than useful, his etymologizing sometimes tendentious, but his body of work can be said to have maintained the momentum of slang lexicography through the mid-20th century. He has that rare accolade: like Webster his name became an eponym. The last edition of the *DSUE* appeared in 1984; an Americanized edition, from 1945 onwards, appeared in 2005 edited by Tom Dalzell (USA) and Terry Victor (UK). This author's single-volume *Cassell Dictionary of Slang* appeared in 1998; two revised editions followed in 2005 and 2008. The multi-volumed 'historical' expansion, *Green's Dictionary of Slang*, was published in 2010.

America

Slang is an urban phenomenon. Modern America seems quintessentially urban; 19th-century America was not.

Two men, Thomas Mount, whose *Confessions* appeared in 1791, after he had been hanged for burglary in Newport, RI, and Henry Tufts, whose *Narrative of the Life, Adventures, Travels and Sufferings of Henry Tufts* was published in 1807, point forward to the many dictionaries of cant, criminal confessionals, and the vast selection of American crime-related material available in both fiction and non-fiction.

'At my desire,' wrote Mount (or the hack who penned the text), 'the language and songs of the American Flash Company are published to inform the world at large of how wicked that company is and how necessary it is to root them up like so many thorns and briars.' Mount's glossary runs to 108 entries. Half is well-established English cant and can be found in Grose.

The 19th century saw only one major American slang dictionary: the *Vocabulum* (1859) by the New York chief of police, G. W. Matsell. (Its only possible predecessor is a short glossary appended by Edward Judson to his *Mysteries and Miseries of New York* (1848).) Some of his vocabulary was undoubtedly taken from Egan's Grose, and the canting songs he appends seem to have come from London and not New York. But Matsell was far from wholly dependent on other lexicographers. Much of the work was local and original. To look only at the letter 'B'—with some 127 headwords—one finds 39 terms (nearly one-third of the letter) for which, to date, his is the first recorded example.

There were other slang dictionaries, but none of major worth. Alfred Trumble's 1881 *Slang Dictionary of New York, London and Paris* was a word-for-word plagiarism of Matsell. The

American Slang Dictionary by the Chicago journalist James
Maitland appeared in 1891. His aim, as stated, was 'to include
what may be termed the slang of the Anglo-Saxon, whether he
dwell in London or New York, in Chicago or Sydney'. This
involved a great deal of introductory self-promotion, but the
dictionary made no real mark.

Matsell was a policeman who dealt in slang as a sideline; his
nearest rivals came in two lexicographers who ostensibly
specialized in what they termed *Americanisms*. Both John Bartlett
and M. Schele de Vere found that to tackle local coinages was
inevitably to tackle slang. Their books, appearing respectively in
1849 (with revisions in 1861 and 1877) and 1872, are as
comprehensive repositories of the register's developments as
anything produced at the time.

The 20th century hosted an explosion of US slang lexicons. Many
of these, such as Jackson and Hellyer's *Vocabulary of Criminal
Slang* (1914), Godfrey Irwin's *American Tramp and Underworld
Slang* (1931), Hyman E. Goldin's *Dictionary of American
Underworld Lingo* (1950), or the wide-ranging specialist work of
David Maurer, published in *American Speech* and elsewhere, point
up the wide variety of US criminal slang. More general works
include Maurice H. Weseen's *Dictionary of American Slang*
(1934), Berrey and Van der Bark's *American Thesaurus of Slang*
(1942, 1952), Harold Wentworth and Stuart Berg Flexner's
Dictionary of American Slang (1960, 1975), and pre-eminently
Jonathan Lighter's tragically unfinished multi-volume work, *The
Historical Dictionary of American Slang* (1994, 1997). Specialist
works abound, especially as regards such sources of slang as the
campus, African-American speech, drugs, and war. Among these
are Connie Eble's series of Campus Slang glossaries (1972 et seq.);
the works of Edith A. Folb (*Runnin' Down Some Lines*, 1980),
Geneva Smitherman (*Black Talk*, 1994), and most recently Maciej
Widawski, *African American Slang: A Linguistic Description*
(2015); Richard A. Spears (*The Slang and Jargon of Drink and*

Drugs, 1986) and Gregory C. Clark (*Words of the Vietnam War*, 1990). Tom Dalzell, co-editor of the revised *DSUE*, has written several specialist dictionaries including *From Flappers to Rappers* (1999) and *Vietnam War Slang* (2014). For a pair of highly focused works, looking at very different topics, see Michael Adams's *Slayer Slang: A* Buffy the Vampire Slayer *Lexicon* (2004) and Jesse Sheidlower's *The F-Word* (3rd edn, 2009), an exhaustive assessment of *fuck*.

On-line dictionaries

The Internet is now the go-to source for information and on-line reference replaces traditional print. There is quantity, but the question for users must be, is there also quality? The primary on-line slang dictionary, the *Urban Dictionary*, is created by its users. Its list of headwords runs into millions, its etymologies and definitions are based on a display of rival icons—thumbs-up or thumbs-down—which display the users' opinions on what has been included. There is no editorial judgement of the accuracy and pertinence of these opinions, and thus no attempt to impose the level of authority that traditionalists would say should be expected of a dictionary if it is to be of real use. In many case the words submitted, several thousand a day, represent nonce-uses, the terminology of an individual or a small group. *Urban Dictionary* represents, some would claim, the wisdom of the crowd; critics would suggest its futility.

The question, again relevant Internet-wide, is whether there remains a role for top-down authority, even in reference works, the primary role of which is to answer questions with a trustworthy 'yes' or 'no'. Slang dictionaries, one might suggest, are built upon an innate paradox: the lexicographer wishes to offer authority but is mining, displaying, and explaining a lexis the entire function of which is to challenge authority in every form. Johnson's decision to use only the 'best' writers as evidence of usage, and the arguments that the original *OED* faced—to what extent one might depend on the verity of non-canonical sources, such as the newspapers that James Murray saw as so useful a source—do not enter the slang equation. It is some time since slang was seen as alien to 'quality literature' and some of the 'best' writers now use slang without hesitation, but the main sources are definitely non-canonical. The opposite of the 'best' may not be the 'worst', but it is definitely the popular, even populist. That, after all, is where slang's origins lie and the world most of its speakers inhabit. Nor, any longer, does it come from print alone.

The Internet provides a seeming infinity of material, and the slang gatherer must look beyond books, and beyond narratives, to lyrics, scripts, blogs, tweets, and so on. Slang has always been found outside books, for instance in songs and ballads, but never in such profusion.

Can these new sources be trusted? One can use the Internet's search functions to find evidence of use; the more so, the better one may prove the popularity and stability of a term. This is the traditional way: the slips that the *OED* amassed, the file cards of later dictionaries, the databases and corpora of modernity. The more instances, the more 'real' the word. This does not stand for user-generated material. Not quite as challenging as a collection of family 'slang', when every family, often inspired by infant mispronunciation, generates a micro-vocabulary for domestic use, the submissions by users represent a near infinity of niche vocabularies. Unconfined by space or worries as to 'authority', on-line dictionaries can allow everyone their say. The formal lexicographer, whether, albeit decreasingly often, in print or on-line, must still make decisions. The question emerges: can we still talk of 'slang' or is the reality a vast confection of 'slangs'?

Chapter 9
The future of slang

In common with much else, slang's future is interwoven with our new connected, digitized world. What will this mean for slang? Are we, any longer, able safely to talk of 'slang' as a discrete language group or are the varieties of non-standard language to become subject to the promotion of niche interests, in this case forms of speech, that the digital world encourages? Finally, is the nature and content of slang, or slangs, due to change? Of slang's continuing existence, there is no doubt. The question that cannot be avoided is what, now, makes up 'slang'?

Does 'slang' exist?

So slippery indeed is slang that one may even wonder whether it really exists as a single, identifiable register and accompanying lexis. The questions as to its boundaries, whether one can properly isolate it from colloquial or standard, which have made it so problematic a concept for linguists, have now begun to bedevil the lexicographers who hitherto tended to sidestep them as they created what were cheerfully termed 'Dictionaries of Slang'. To an extent Eric Partridge, whose lexicon's full title, coined in 1937 and persisting until 1984, embraced not merely slang but 'unconventional English, colloquialisms and catchphrases, fossilized jokes and puns, general nicknames, vulgarisms and such Americanisms as have been naturalised', was the first to recognize the problem. For critics this diluted the lexis he offered, and the work is undoubtedly uneven, with a sense that as edition followed edition the dictionary was becoming too much of an inchoate grab-bag of what its author had stumbled upon.

Partridge, and his American contemporaries, like their predecessors, could still see 'slang' as a unit. The 'unconventional language' and the rest was an appendage, not a variation nor alternative. Even if for all of Partridge's supposed rules of qualification, 'slang' was ultimately something, to quote Michael Adams once more, that one 'knew when one saw it', it was assumed that Partridge and others did see it, and what they saw was therefore slang. One might dispute the details, typically his cavalier approach to etymology, but not the bigger picture.

For Partridge slang came primarily from the white working class and their criminal cousins. He combed the canonical run of glossaries and dictionaries, as remains an inescapable task, and duly remade their lists among his own. He excluded America, preferring to confect, as time passed, a somewhat more substantial 'Canadian' lexis that might truly have been the case. He was unhappy with the modern young, with rock 'n' roll, with hippies, and with drugs. He was happiest with the armed forces with whom he had served in two world wars. He worked, every day, in the old British Museum Reading Room. He knew, and could only know, print.

Slang, like the rest of the world, lives in 'interesting times'. A mixed blessing (and a Chinese curse). The *Urban Dictionary*'s constant accretion of new material, even if quality is regularly outpaced by quantity, is probably the most 'real-time' approach to non-standard language possible: the print dictionary is out of date as soon as it is published; its digital successor has no such problems.

Critics, traditionalists, deplore its lack of dependable authority—so many cooks that it is barely possible to see the broth, let alone ascertain whether it is appetizing or spoiled—and wonder, deluged by so great a plenitude of information, whether how much, if any, of what it offers can be qualified as slang.

Does that matter? Its users may offer widely varying definitions for a single word, but none questions the term's inclusion. The website no longer promotes itself as a 'slang dictionary'. Its credo—'define your world'—sums up its driving force and hundreds of thousands of contributors seem keen to do so. Its creator has explained that he set up *UD* in 1999 because his generation, then around 20, could no longer tolerate traditional dictionaries attempting to set down what 'their' language meant.

It is, perhaps, a generational standpoint that will influence whether one feels that this is a positive move, or otherwise. On one side one has the slang dictionary's traditional role: laying down lexical law, a law that, if undoubtedly debatable, is as true of slang dictionaries as of standard. On the other, one has a genuine attempt to set down as much as possible of the non-standard language that people actually use as can be done. Given the boundlessness of cyberspace, this plan need have no end. Depending on one's viewpoint, one may judge this to be a featureless, untrustworthy maelstrom, fascinating, revelatory, amusing, but in no way of practical use; or one may see it as the way ahead.

What *UD* does, and this has not often been attempted before, and never, ever on this scale, is to hand the work of lexicography over to those who are involved hands-on with their subject. Like Partridge when he recoiled from recreational drug users, all of whom were simply labelled 'addicts' irrespective of their stimulant of choice, this author is very far away from those whose language he attempts to corral. This is often the case: those who use the words have neither time nor desire to analyse them. Those who perform that task are more than likely to be observing from a distance. Ideally, the enthusiasm of the coiners could be coupled with the rigour of the collectors.

Which still does not answer the question: does slang exist? In 2013, researching a paper on Multi-Ethnic London English, the blend of rap, Jamaican patois, home-grown Londonisms, and mainstream American and British slang that makes up UK slang's cutting edge, I read an interview with one teenage Londoner, fluent in the style. How would he describe his language? Slang. And would he use it forever? No. So what would he speak as an adult? Cockney. That 'Cockney' is what many might term slang was out of the equation. To him that was 'standard'. But then for the moment what he termed 'slang' was his current standard too, even if he recognized that it was alien to the wider world.

That is his opinion. His world. He is hardly unique. The traditional slang collector has always been forced back on the general, on 'slang'. This might have been possible in the UK, where London still dominates, but was always dubious in the USA, where New York, while vastly influential, has no monopoly. In either case the lexicographer has been forced to turn a wilfully blind eye. Print, with its restrictions of space and the dictates of a publishing house, has allowed for this, rendered it inevitable. The excuse no longer exists.

The collection of slang, the lexis of 'loose talk', has always involved a number of loose ends. As soon as glossaries moved beyond cant, and took on aspects of 'civilian' slang, one can sense that what was offered was far from all of what existed. Research was not systematized, the collector offered what was found. Reading the manuscript notes that Captain Grose interleaved in his own copy of his 1785 dictionary, paving the way for its successor of 1788, one finds a wide range of material: the names of social clubs, a number of taboo terms (some of which would never be published, such as *A—e man*, defined punningly as 'an invader of the back settlements'), words launched by current events, the names of drinks, proverbial phrases, and more. One senses today that all ends are loose. To look no further than a single city, there are differences not merely as to area, but also as to the language of estates or housing projects.

There remain certain subsets for which boundaries can be drawn. These are the informal languages that develop within a certain occupation. Not technicalities, but job-specific slangs. There is still 'cant', the language of criminals, but that might equally be seen as a jargon, as might the 'slangs' of drug users, members of the forces, and others whose purpose-specific vocabularies have, at least in part, appeared in the slang dictionaries. Some slang lexicographers have chosen to include the language of major sports, others that of certain of the media. It is a slippery slope and one tips too easily into a dictionary of occupational languages. In any case, there exists enough 'mainstream' slang, the non-conventional language of everyday life, to fill any dictionary. But a fissiparous world, offering a showcase to every niche thanks to the Internet and to social media, makes it increasingly hard to qualify slang as a bounded, single entity, as could (or certainly as believed) Francis Grose or Eric Partridge.

A slang corpus?

How best might one approach so substantial a lexis? Current lexicography, at least as regards dictionaries of contemporary language and those created to attend the demands of EFL/ESL, are now orientated to the evidence provided by the vast assemblages of evidential material provided by a number of linguistic corpora. These show the way language is used and provide the bases upon which dictionary entries and their nuanced senses can be created, based not on what is inevitably a random selection of citations, but on the hard evidence of the way a given term is used 'live'. There does not yet, and perhaps may never, exist a corpus focused wholly on slang. This may be for scholarly reasons, perhaps for economic ones. It may even be simple oversight. The wide use of slang in fiction and across the media surely ensures that the material would be available; but it still remains comparatively limited and might not generate the hundreds of millions of examples required for useful analysis. It should also be noted that corpora require a printed record from which to extract material. Far from all slang is recorded in this way and much, of course, remains on the spoken level. Geared as they are to contemporary usage, corpora also fail to help dictionaries that look backwards. Yet the idea should not be dismissed. One could suggest that the *Urban Dictionary* might provide a possible seedbed for launching such a slang corpus, but the idea has yet to take root.

Girl talk

Slang is traditionally a male preserve and much of what has been suggested about slang's traditional themes offers a male viewpoint. This may be changing. It is hard to pin down historical female slang usage: whores had slang, chorus girls presumably used it, flappers certainly did, some of the raunchiest blues singers were women. But use is not coinage and it is challenging to separate the two. The feisty British 'ladettes' of the 1990s were notably foul-mouthed, but used a male lexis. The Internet may well be offering a revolution here as elsewhere. Social media, where young women dominate communication, is changing the rules. Its language—*totes*, *adorbs*, *on fleek*—is a female construct. Nor is obscenity mandatory. Women can use it, as noted, but, as these samples suggest, social media's 'girl talk' looks in other directions, and, flouting another of slang's male conventions, appears generally positive.

Where are we going?

The more slang changes, the more it stays the same. If one accepts that there is an innate desire to play with words, and to voice attitudes in an unfettered manner, however reprehensible that manner may sometimes be seen to be, then slang will continue to provide the means. Those who feel that its vast lists of synonyms have surely exhausted our inventiveness will be disappointed, or perhaps relieved: slang will continue on its path of self-invention. Secrecy is something of an illusion, but slang neologizing will continue (Figure 10). Each new generation will guarantee that.

On a lexical level, what we shall see is more of the same: the same themes, the same preoccupations, the same images. Sex, drugs, and rock 'n' roll. Human feelings rather than artificially dictated ones. Slang, its hands full dealing with the concrete, is not likely to take on abstraction.

On a social level a qualification as 'slang' will be increasingly adjudicated by those who use it. The concepts of 'right' and 'wrong' no longer play a part. Not good, not bad, not 'standard',

10. 'The Slang Duellists' by Isaac Cruikshank (1807). Not that much slang—'cannister' for pistol and 'bread-basket' for stomach—but highly indicative of the language such aristocratic, but far from professionally criminal 'flash gentry' might have used at the time.

and not 'slang' but the strings of letters that when spoken or written serve us as communication. Of course this has always been the underpinning reality of slang, but the extent of possibilities has never been so great.

If this is the situation, it is hard to see much justification for creating rules as regards what is or is not 'slang'. They seem artificial, desperate, a drive to control and thus defang. If 'slang' embodies our innate rebelliousness (the undying, if not always expressed, desire to say 'no') then how can it not reject the strait-jacket. We are moving away from top-down diktats—in language as elsewhere. If we must define then I suggest that the words we term slang are seen simply as representatives of that subset of English spoken in the context of certain themes, by certain people, in certain circumstances. The illustration of what those themes, people, and circumstances are has been the premise of this brief overview. This is broad-brush, but such is the point: what can be shorthanded as 'slang' is simply one more form of the language. It is not mandatory and codes can and will be switched. That the themes, and our way of addressing them, are still considered 'improper' makes them even more alluring. This is the language we use to talk about the things that make us tick. If it is a thing apart then that exclusion comes with the territory that it has chosen, and the walls are erected not by 'slang' and its speakers but by those who find that territory—for all that it is so very human—problematic.

Further reading

A number of books, especially slang dictionaries and glossaries, have been noted within the text. In addition readers might like to consider the following.

General studies

Adams, Michael *Slang: The People's Poetry* (OUP, 2009).

Coleman, Julie *A History of Cant and Slang Dictionaries* (4 vols OUP, 2004–).

Coleman, Julie *The Story of Slang* (OUP, 2011).

Green, Jonathon *Language: 500 Years of the Vulgar Tongue* (Atlantic, 2014).

Partridge, Eric *Slang To-Day & Yesterday* (RKP, 1933).

Readers are also directed to the introductions of recent major slang dictionaries, e.g. those of Jonathan Lighter's *Historical Dictionary of American Slang* (Random House, 1994–), Tom Dalzell and Terry Victor's *New Partridge Dictionary of Slang and Unconventional English* (Routledge, 2008), and this author's *Green's Dictionary of Slang* (Chambers, 2010).

Topical studies

While general histories of slang remain rare, specific aspects of the topic have been covered more widely. These titles cover some of slang's primary areas, but a good deal more material, both academic and general, exists and can be tracked down.

Allen, Irving Lewis *The City in Slang* (OUP USA, 1993).

Bardsley, Diana *Book of New Zealand Words* (Te Papa Press, 2013).

Eble, Connie *Slang & Sociability* (University of North Carolina Press, 1996).

Moore, Bruce *Speaking our Language: The Story of Australian English* (OUP Australia, 2008).

Sheidlower, Jesse *The F Word* (3rd edn OUP, 2009).

Widawski, Maciej *African American Slang: A Linguistic Description* (CUP, 2015).

Index

Page numbers in italics refer to illustrations.

Slang

Slang